THE ART OF P

THE
ART OF
PERFORMANCE

HEINRICH SCHENKER

Edited by Heribert Esser

Translated by Irene Schreier Scott

UNIVERSITY PRESS

OXFORD

UNIVERSITY PRESS

Oxford   New York

Auckland   Bangkok   Buenos Aires   Cape Town   Chennai
Dar es Salaam   Delhi   Hong Kong   Istanbul   Karachi   Kolkata
Kuala Lumpur   Madrid   Melbourne   Mexico City   Mumbai   Nairobi
São Paulo   Shanghai   Singapore   Taipei   Tokyo   Toronto

and an associated company in Berlin

First published in 2000 by Oxford University Press, Inc.
198 Madison Avenue, New York, New York 10016

www.oup.com

First issued as an Oxford University Press paperback, 2002

Oxford is a registered trademark of Oxford University Press

Library of Congress Cataloging-in-Publication Data
Schenker, Heinrich, 1868–1935
[Kunst des Vortrags. English]
The art of performance : Heinrich Schenker ;
edited by Heribert Esser ;
translated by Irene Schreier Scott.
p.   cm.
An unfinished work edited from the author's papers in the
New York Public Library and the University of California at Riverside.
Includes bibliographical references and index.
Contents: Musical composition and performance—Mode of notation and performance—
The technique of playing the piano—Nonlegato—Legato—Staccato—
Fingering—Dynamics—Tempo and tempo modifications—Rests—
The performance of older music—On practicing.
ISBN 0-19-512254-2; ISBN 0-19-515151-8 (pbk.)
1. Piano—Performance.
2. Piano music—Interpretation (Phrasing, dynamics, etc.).
I. Esser, Heribert.   II. Title.
MT220.S24513   2000
786.2'193—dc21   99-10082

1 3 5 7 9 8 6 4 2

Printed in the United States of America
on acid-free paper

Contents

Translator's Introduction

THIS IS THE FIRST publication of Heinrich Schenker's *The Art of Performance*. That its appearance is in translation should not come as a surprise. Interest in Schenker's work is liveliest in the English-speaking world at present and is no longer confined to theoreticians. This practical volume, then, may serve as an introduction to Schenker, particularly directed to practicing musicians.

My personal introduction to the substance of *The Art of Performance* antedates by many years my awareness of its existence. By chance my first piano teacher was Moriz Violin, a wonderfully gifted pianist who also composed. Violin was Heinrich Schenker's younger colleague and closest friend, in whom Schenker confided and with whom he shared his musical ideas. Having intuitively assimilated these concepts, Violin imparted them in his own teaching along with a special, unforgettable approach to the piano. From the age of six, therefore, I was shown a natural way of playing entirely at one with the music and, perhaps because Violin had never taught a child before, I was spared any of the "piano methods" most beginners are taught.

Later, in my college years, I studied with Oswald Jonas (who had meanwhile become my stepfather). Counterpoint, figured bass, and analysis played a considerable role, but I think it is fair to say that what he cared about most of all were our lessons at the piano, with detailed coaching of every nuance. Certainly he pointed out the unique musical content of each work and, in the most memorable moments, we made new discoveries; the emphasis, however, was on musical expression.

Heinrich Schenker's deep concern for performance—for the execution of the works his analytical insights illuminated so profoundly —has become widely recognized. It is known that his own students were for the greater part taught at the piano, and anyone who has overheard a Schenker student in the process of analyzing a piece of music—probing, playing a segment of a phrase over and over again, emphasizing first one, then another note or group of notes—is aware that the actual sound of the music and its appropriate expression are essential to Schenker's approach to music. In addition, the sections on performance in most of his writings and the many allusions to a forthcoming publication of *Die Kunst des Vortrags* in journals and books by Schenker scholars have already served to introduce this volume. But music students and musicians with no direct experience with Schenker—and this translation is meant every bit as much for them as for the initiated—may still be surprised at the practical, detailed technical advice given by the theoretician they have only associated with apparently esoteric, abstract graphic analyses.

The genesis of *The Art of Performance (Die Kunst des Vortrags)* has been described in detail in the editor's introduction. When I was first asked to translate it and reread the manuscript (not yet in its current form) it seemed like an old friend, and I even queried the usefulness of its publication at a time when, I thought, many of its ideas had become widespread. Since then, however, I have taught a wide variety of students, and I find that the basic approach to the piano taken by most students is very different indeed from the one that spoke to me in a familiar language from the pages of *Vortrag*. Certainly, pianists need the ability to play many types and styles of music, including those unequivocally rejected by Schenker. But the repertoire from, say, Bach to Brahms (as well as much else!) is played convincingly, with its own appropriate expression, only when it sings and breathes. The means, the motions, the physical approach described in the text that follows can point the way to music making that is immediate, alive, spontaneous, and yet controlled. In our more and more programmed world, such music making becomes profoundly meaningful.

I have been helped in the process of preparing this translation by the many friends, colleagues, and students whose enthusiasm for the project was an inspiration. Special thanks to John Rothgeb, Carl Schachter, and William Rothstein for their valuable, expert suggestions; to Robert Lang and Sidney Berger of the University Library,

University of California, Riverside, for their generosity in putting all the materials in the Oswald Jonas Memorial Collection needed for the illustrations reproduced here, at my disposal; to Maribeth Payne of Oxford University Press and her staff for making the publication possible, with special appreciation for Cynthia Garver who patiently and with expertise helped overcome obstacles; to Andrew Lee for his painstaking, careful work in preparing all the examples on the computer; and to my husband, Dana Scott, for his advice on sensitive linguistic questions and for giving unstintingly of his time in helping in the final stages of organizing the manuscript. I also particularly want to thank Richard Goode for his interest in this work. Without his gentle nudging when the preparation seemed to take forever, the book might still not be in print.

I am especially happy that Oxford University Press undertook this publication during 1997, the centenary of Oswald Jonas's birth. The memory of his boundless enthusiasm for music was the inspiration for my part in the realization of this project, one particularly close to his heart.

Pittsburgh   I.S.S.
March 1998

Editor's Introduction

IN THE PREFACE TO his book on Beethoven's Ninth Symphony (1912), Heinrich Schenker writes (p. 8): "Under the above-mentioned performance rubric I have endeavored, without intending to encroach on the territory of a monograph 'Die Kunst des Vortrags' to be published in the foreseeable future, to set forth performance instructions insofar as possible in general principles and rules."

Where is this monograph? It was never completed. Schenker had begun sketching the projected *The Art of Performance* systematically in July 1911 but interrupted work on it a few weeks later. (See "Sources and Editorial Procedure.") After some two years he took this material out of his desk, but only to "check through it and improve its organization." A considerable part of the usable material had already been included in earlier publications: in *A Contribution to the Study of Ornamentation* (1904), in *J. S. Bach's Chromatic Fantasy and Fugue* (1909), and in the monograph previously quoted.

We do not know why Schenker did not continue work on this project begun so energetically. It is hard to believe that problems intrinsic to the material were responsible. One might rather agree with the reasons given by Oswald Jonas in an introduction written in 1958 to a never-realized version of the work:

"In the above-mentioned preface [to the Ninth Symphony] it furthermore says "I believe, incidentally, that I am the first to consider similar principles at all applicable to a material that appears to be in a constant state of flux. Naturally I have also endeavored, however, to provide the rules in all cases with their psychological foundation as thoroughly as possible, in order to shield them from even the appearance of being merely accidental and arbitrary. For this reason the rubric of performance would have automatically required still more exhaustive treatment; but in view of the greater importance of the revelation of content, I had to satisfy myself with less extensive commentary." Herein, simultaneously, lies the explanation for the fact that "The Art of Performance" remained a fragment: it was the "theory of organic unity in the musical work of art"—the idea of the "*Ursatz* and its prolongations"—which Schenker considered it his mission to present and whose formulation became the uppermost aim of his life's work. Added to this his practical activity as teacher, his battle against the obfuscation of source material (the entire current awareness of the significance of the manuscript for the preparation of the printed text, after all, essentially stems from Schenker's attempts and admonitions)—if one weighs all this it becomes understandable that the "Vortrag," along with many other projects, had to take second place in his life-plan and to remain a fragment.

Many years later, on December 6, 1930, Schenker dictates to his wife, Jeanette, the following diary entry: "Ordered 'Vortrag' and supplied it with a sort of Index. Thus only the book itself remains, destined to be a diversion and distraction from the difficulties of *Free Composition*." He had not completely lost sight of the old papers and their questions during the past twenty years; for this we have proof in the abundant number of notes that are collected in B of "Sources and Editorial Procedure." (See this chapter for this and all following references to the Schenker materials.) Now, apparently, he had come to the firm conclusion to take up that large piece of work once again and to bring it to some sort of resolution. But this was not to happen. Indeed, Schenker did finish *Free Composition* to the extent that it could be published—shortly after his death—in 1935; but the book *The Art of Performance* remained unpublished. Even in its fragmentary state, however, *The Art of Performance* presents its material in such an individual, unconventional manner and contains such a wealth of valuable, stimulating ideas and suggestions that the posthumous publication seems more than justified—even if one knows that it can never be the "book" Schenker intended to write.

"*Entwurf (Versuch) einer Lehre vom Vortrag. Ein Beitrag zur Verbesserung /Reform des Klavierspiels im Besonderen*" [Draft of (Essay on) a Study of Performance. A Contribution to the Improvement/Reform of Piano Playing in Particular]—this annotation written on a scrap of paper represents Schenker's early searching for a title for the work. (See Plate 1.) It was intended to echo another *Essay*: that of his admired and beloved C. P. E. Bach *On the True Art of Playing Keyboard Instruments*—a work that Schenker knew as no one else did and which is one of the foundations for his own efforts. At the same time, we realize why the *Vortrag* is addressed almost exclusively to pianists. The pianist is the one Schenker considers the most in danger of falling into the ways of poor, miscalculated performance, since for the purely mechanical activation of the keys none of the natural constraints apply to which singers or wind players are subject by the need to breathe or string players by the motions of bowing. Schenker does not tire of admonishing the pianist to "breathe," to bring to his eyes and ears the model of the human voice for "singing" playing and "speaking" articulation. In doing this Schenker continually holds up the example given by J. S. Bach, C. P. E. Bach, Mozart, or Beethoven.

By abandoning his original suggestions for a title in favor of the more general *The Art of Performance* Schenker appears to modify his stance; but since by far the greatest number of examples are taken from the piano literature—especially by Beethoven and Chopin—he betrays his true intention. It would of course be entirely wrong to attribute this slant toward the piano to one-sidedness on the author's part: what he says about the piano here can easily be applied to other instruments. Or better, in Schenker's own words in *The Masterwork in Music*, vol.1, p. 48:

> Whether written for organ, clavier or violin, music is above all music (when it is good) and all instrumental peculiarities are through its common characteristics far more unified than they are separated by variations in the constructions of the tool. And should we wish to contemplate an "ideal instrument" that in a sense underlies all actual ones, it would have to be the human voice, which, as the most natural artistic tool, fills all diminutions and voice-leading prolongations with its soul, with the laws of its performance, however they are developed and to whatever instrument they are applied. . . . That is confirmed by the history of music as well.

Even though the book on performance never took shape under Schenker's hands, we have been somewhat compensated by the sections on performance he added to his analyses. Outstanding examples of this are Beethoven, Sonata op. 57 (*Tonwille*, vol. 1, 1924); Brahms, Variations on a Theme by Handel, op. 24 (*Tonwille*, vol. 8/9, 1924); Mozart, Symphony in G Minor, K. 550 (*The Masterwork in Music, vol.2*). The fingerings in Schenker's edition of the complete Beethoven piano sonatas alone represent an advanced school of performance; they are not "explained," but they lead the player compellingly in the right direction—as Carl Schachter has convincingly demonstrated in his introduction to the English edition. Furthermore, there are virtually inexhaustible riches contained in Schenker's own music library (Oster Collection [OC] and Oswald Jonas Memorial Collection [OJMC]) in the form of the most detailed remarks regarding performance, which he entered into the scores. William Rothstein's extensive study "Heinrich Schenker as an Interpreter of Beethoven's Piano Sonatas" affords us a tantalizing glimpse. And last but not least, the Lesson Books should be mentioned, in which Schenker gives examples of the principles of good performance in relation to the successful or unsuccessful achievements of his students (OC, files 3, 16, 30, 38).

Of particular interest are Schenker's remarks on musical performance by artists of his own time. They can be found in the music reviews he published in various periodicals between 1891 and 1901, collected by Hellmut Federhofer in *Heinrich Schenker als Essayist und Kritiker*. Even more revealing are diary entries that followed concerts Schenker had attended or radio broadcasts he had heard. Oswald Jonas, who owned the diaries (now part of OJMC), gave several excerpts from these as far back as 1964 in his paper "Heinrich Schenker und grosse Interpreten." Further material can be found in Federhofer's biography of Schenker. Of course we see in all these testimonials the high demands and absolute standards we have come to expect of Schenker. But some will be surprised by how many artists won his approval and, often, his enthusiastic praise.

It was Schenker's unwavering conviction that only proper understanding of the content of the musical work of art could lead to its true execution. So it was only logical that, with the continuing development of his "theory of organic unity," performance demands also took on new dimensions. For this interaction of theory and practice it is noteworthy that a number of notes can be found in B that were originally clearly intended for what was later to become *Free Composition* but then were relegated to *The Art of Performance*— at least this must be concluded from the alteration of the heading in some annotations. Let me quote one of these that with one stroke clearly illuminates Schenker's intentions:

> What is *practical* in this book [i.e., *Free Composition*] lies less in the education to genius, which is anyhow impossible, than in instructing composers in need of assistance to attain the means of extending the content; most *decisively*, however, it may serve the art of performance: here the book may point the way to those absolute solutions that result compellingly from the unity of synthesis. Thus particularly the art of performance, which up to now everyone might practice according to his personal conception, can here solidly find its own ground; for one who can correctly read [i.e., understand] a masterwork can surely summon the reproductive means of bringing it to life. This part, then, can absolutely be taught and learned—whereas instruction in progressing from background to foreground, to diminutions in the foreground, must cease at the limits of talent.

Schenker does his utmost to guide the interpreter. In *The Masterwork in Music*, vol. 1, we read on p. 37 how he imagines this—at least concerning dynamics:

> In my forthcoming treatise, "The Art of Performance," it will be systematically shown for the first time that dynamics, like voice-leading and diminution, are organized according to structural levels, genealogically as it were. For each level of voice-leading, whether background or foreground, and for each level of diminution, there is a corresponding dynamic level of the first order, second order, and so forth. In the Foreground Graph, these various levels are shown separately: the primary dynamic shading, which belongs to the first level of voice-leading and diminution is indicated, while the inner shadings, those that apply to diminutions of the third order that emerge only in the Foreground Graph, are given above the stave.

In an essay, "Schenker's Theory of Levels and Musical Performance," Charles Burkhart deals with this concept among others. One has to agree with his feeling that Schenker silently gave up the idea at some stage.

However it may be, the implications of these and other theoretical insights from Schenker's later period are not apparent in *The Art of Performance*, if for no other reason than that the greatest part of the material stems from a time before their formulation. Also in B there are only a handful of examples influenced by these insights, and the explanations given along with them are so sparse that, for a thorough understanding, a commentary would be required that would by far exceed the framework of this volume. Therefore, these examples have not been included herewith.

At this point I would like to commemorate the man whose name has been mentioned repeatedly and without whom this publication would hardly have come about: Oswald Jonas. Only a few months after Schenker's death, Mrs. Schenker allowed Jonas to inspect his teacher's *Nachlass*. Jonas immediately recognized the extraordinary significance of the material for *The Art of Performance*. But only after the hiatus due to the upheaval before and during World War II, after his emigration and the gradual rebuilding of his life, could he begin the extremely laborious task of deciphering and interpreting Schenker's notes. Bringing the results of these efforts (C and D of "Sources and Editorial Procedure") into a shape appropriate for publication was a task to which Jonas dedicated himself with my assistance during his European visits in the 1950s. The manuscript we produced jointly, at that time in the form of a "lexicon," finally landed, in a roundabout way, with Schenker's old publisher, Universal Edition Vienna; it then took Universal Edition a quarter of a century—not to publish it!

Although I decided to give up the idea of a lexicon and chose a basically different format for the current publication, nevertheless I am deeply indebted to Oswald Jonas for his preliminary work. To him, friend and teacher, to his memory this book is dedicated in gratitude.

This book is the first major publication to come out of Heinrich Schenker's *Nachlass*. That it can be presented now, nearly ninety years after its conception and more than sixty years after the death of its author, gives hope that it may stimulate interest in further publications out of the wealth of yet untapped treasures.

Wolfenbüttel   H. E.
September 1997

Sources and Editorial Procedure

The Schenker Nachlass

[OC] The Oster Collection, New York Public Library.

> R. Kosovsky, *The Oster Collection: Papers of H. Schenker. A Finding List*. New York Public Library, 1990. (Hereafter: *Finding List*)

[OJMC] The Oswald Jonas Memorial Collection, Rivera Library, University of California at Riverside.

> R. Lang and J. Kunselman, *H. Schenker, O. Jonas, M. Violin: A Checklist of Manuscripts and Other Papers in the Oswald Jonas Memorial Collection*. University of California Press, 1994. (Hereafter: *Checklist*)

Source Materials

A. *Vom Vortrag*

> MS in Jeanette Schenker's handwriting, with additions by Heinrich Schenker: 84 pp., numbered 1–86 (3 pp. are numbered twice; 1 p. was added).

> OJMC box 18, folder 10. *Checklist*, p. 51.

H. Schenker, entries in his journal. OJMC boxes 1–4. *Checklist*, pp. 3–5
Relevant Quotations:

> 1 July 1911. Initial work on the essay "Kunst des Vortrags."
>
> 13 July 1911. Except for a few notes, organized "Kunst des Vortrags" for the first time (for the present!).
>
> 29 July 1911. Dictated "Kunst des Vortrags" to the end.
>
> 7 July 1913. Checked through the monograph on performance and improved organization . . .

B. Fragmente und Notizen *(Fragments and Notes)*

All written by Heinrich and (from dictation) by Jeanette Schenker. Some dated, other material in used envelopes or between pages of periodicals, thereby allowing their time of origin or organization to be inferred: 1914–32, most of the notes probably 1926–29. OJMC box 21, folders 7–21. *Checklist*, pp. 64–65.

C. *Schenker* Vortrag. *Erster Entwurf und Ergänzungen (First draft and supplement). Typescript by O. Jonas.*

First Draft: Copy of A with insertions of text and examples from B; additional examples and comments by Jonas. Pagination 1–63a.

Supplement: Material from B with additional material by Jonas. Pagination 1–45.

H. Esser. Copy in OC, file 13/5. *Finding List*, pp. 45–46—there mistakenly attributed to Ernst Oster.

D. *Schenker* Vortrag. *Zweiter Entwurf und Ergänzungen*

(Second draft and supplement). Typescript by O. Jonas. Copy of material from B. Pagination 1–38.

OJMC box 57, file 3. *Checklist*, p. 161. Copy in OC, file 13/5. *Finding List*, p. 4—there mistakenly attributed to E. Oster.

History of the Materials

A and B were looked through and put in order by Jeanette Schenker and Oswald Jonas on October 18, 1935. All of this material is mentioned as No. 13 in the Register of Heinrich Schenker's *Nachlass* (copies in OJMC box 35, file 2, *Checklist*, p. 96, and in OC, *Finding List*, p. vi), which was compiled on November 7, 1935; together with the major part of the *Nachlass* it was handed to Ernst Oster by Jeanette Schenker in 1938 and taken by him to New York when he immigrated there during the same year.

After World War II, Jonas received all the material from Oster for the purpose of editing and publishing it. Jonas's first task was the arduous one of deciphering and interpreting the notes casually scribbled on hundreds of slips of paper. Next came the preparation of a kind of fair copy: C and D. This served as a basis for the manuscript prepared for publication that Jonas produced together with me during his European visits from 1955 to 1958. In view of the fragmentary nature of the material, he decided on the form of a lexicon for this: ordering it by key words alphabetically (copy of the MS made by me in OC, file 13/8, *Finding List*, p. 46—there mistakenly attributed to Ernst Oster). Oster participated in the project at a distance by correspondence, giving comments and corrections as well as providing further musical examples, and so forth.

In 1958 a private publisher connected to a German art academy wanted to print the work; however, the difficulty of reproducing the musical examples defeated the attempt. Later Jonas gave the MS to Universal Edition in Vienna, Schenker's old publisher. But not until after Jonas's death in 1978 did Universal Edition decide to publish the work. On the advice of Jonas's stepdaughter and heir, Irene Schreier Scott, Universal Edition approached me with the request to revise the MS.

Thinking about the material again—after more than two decades —I began to have doubts about the usefulness of the lexicon form. These doubts intensified, leading to the decision to make a fundamentally different arrangement of the material. This new approach and the resulting MS were accepted by Universal Edition; it is the work at hand. Why nonetheless, it was not published subsequently by Universal Edition need not be dealt with in the present context.

Editorial Procedure

The fact that the material for *The Art of Performance* consists of fragments cannot and should not be hidden. No segment may be considered as a finished literary product; this is true even for the more extensive chapters in A. In fact, A was dictated by Schenker to his future wife in the short time of only *one* month; it shows all the advantages and disadvantages of such speed. Furthermore, A contains very few practical examples, and of these only two are written out in notation. For the remainder, Schenker contents himself with mere references to specific places or works in general.

B, even more than A, gives an unfinished impression, consisting of hundreds of small scraps of paper (*Zettel*) on which Schenker jotted down his ideas as fast as they occurred to him—often only a few note heads with one single word or musical term as comment or several casually tossed-away unfinished sentences—trains of thought merely hinted at by key words. Only rarely is an idea put into broader context; moreover, we find repetitions, overlaps, corrections, and such in abundance.

The current version of *The Art of Performance* is based on the slightly modified order and structure of the chapters in A; the material from B was incorporated and integrated into the text of A where appropriate. As a basis I used not only Schenker's originals but also and most particularly the extensive preparatory work done by Jonas in C and D.

It is obvious that stylistic problems must occur under these circumstances. Since Schenker would not have considered publishing A or B without a thorough revision, it would have been extraordinarily pedantic to present the sources literally in every detail. I rather felt the need of handling the material with a certain amount of freedom in order to produce a practical, usable edition. May the reader, however, be assured that the text in front of him has as much of Schenker's original wording as possible and as few additions as necessary. Nowhere is an attempt made to "correct" or "improve on" Schenker—not even in the frequently rather incomplete formulations of B. In general, those chapters that contain very few or no examples at all (1, 2, 4, 6, 11, 12) present Schenker's text in its purest form; the chapters with many examples (3, 5, 7, 8, 9, 10) needed the greatest amount of editorial revision.

The small number of notes on the text serve the purpose of giving the reader essential information. There are no notes provided in order to show which editorial decisions were made at any given point; otherwise not only would the size of the book have increased substantially, but also the very "disorder" that the main text attempts to remove would have returned to the bottoms of the pages.

Two chapters contained in A were omitted: "On the Technique of the Piano in Particular" (originally chapter 4) and "On the Degeneracy of the Virtuoso" (originally chapter 12). The appendixes present summaries of both; their unabridged publication is planned in a different context.

The chapter "On Practicing" does not exist in A. Schenker's diverse statements on that subject, which are collected in B, are combined and presented here as chapter 12.

Furthermore, I decided—not lightly—to omit those few examples from B that could only be understood through a thorough knowledge of Schenker's later theories as they are formulated in *Free Composition*. Their inclusion is deemed inappropriate in the more practical context of this work.

Plates

These are some examples of the fragments and notes (see "Source Materials B, *Fragmente und Notizen* [Fragments and Notes]") on which parts of this book are based. Notice that on most of the scraps of paper Schenker indicates that the remark is intended for *The Art of Performance* (*Vortrag* or *Vtg.*).

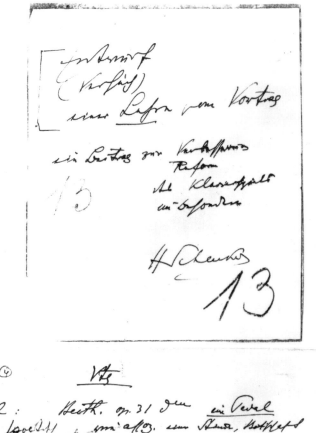

Plate 1 *Top fragment*: This clearly shows Schenker's attempt to formulate a title. (See Editor's Introduction, p. xii.) *Lower fragment*: This concerns Beethoven's use of pedal in Sonata op. 31, no. 2, I. See chapter 3, p. 68.

Plate 2 *Upper right*: This fragment shows Example 3.5 and the remarks that immediately precede it. See chapter 3. *Upper left*: This
fragment (Example 3.9) shows more remarks on the pedal.
Lower right: This fragment shows the source for Example 3.8 that
illustrates the "painting gestures" described in chapter 3, "Piano
Singing." Apparently written on a page-proof fragment.

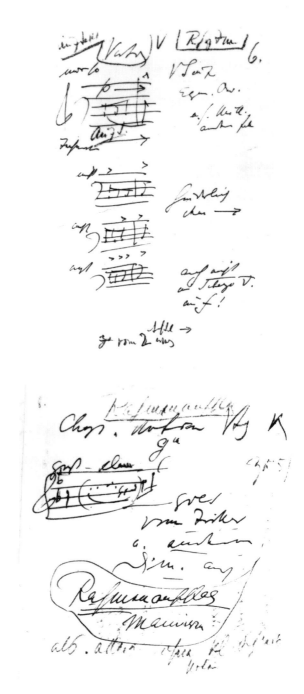

Plate 3 *Top*: The source for Example 9.2. *Bottom*: Remarks on *Rahmenanschlag* that clearly show Example 8.20.

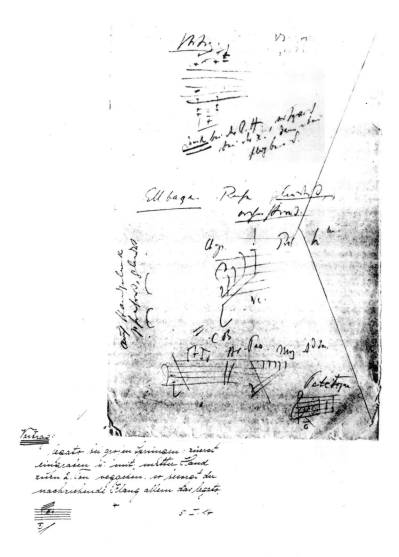

Plate 4 *Upper fragment*: This shows several independent notes on the back of a large envelope. On the bottom the source for Examples 3.20 and 3.21. See chapter 3, *Lower fragment*: In Mrs. Schenker's handwriting, this shows *"legato bei grossen Sprüngen"* (legato in the case of large leaps), et cetera. See chapter 5.

THE ART OF PERFORMANCE

ONE

Musical Composition and Performance

BASICALLY, A COMPOSITION does not require a performance in order to exist. Just as an imagined sound appears real in the mind, the reading of a score is sufficient to prove the existence of the composition. The mechanical realization of the work of art can thus be considered superfluous.

Once a performance does take place, one must realize that thereby new elements are added to a complete work of art: the nature of the instrument that is being played; properties of the hall, the room, the audience; the mood of the performer, technique, et cetera. Now if the composition is to be inviolate, kept as it was prior to the performance, it must not be compromised by these elements (which after all are entirely foreign to it). In other words: those properties must not be given priority. Yet how casually will many an artist sacrifice the work of art—which never should be sacrificed!—to the hall, to the audience, to his fingers! He would do better to immerse himself in the work of art, maintaining its conceptual integrity during the performance. But distorting the composition in performance obviously is easier than fulfilling the very stringent conditions for an appropriate rendition.

To master these difficulties, a superficial acquaintance with the work of art is insufficient. What is essential is a thorough knowledge of all laws of composition. Having enabled the composer to create, these laws, in a different way, will enable the performer to re-create the composition. Inevitably one concludes that a performer who truly re-creates is indeed close to the creator. There is thus no paradox in my claim that it is the great masters of composition who must be considered the best performers! We may be sure that Chopin's renditions were better than Tausig's, and Beethoven's than Bülow's. Strange as it may seem, the better performer is not necessarily the one who has made piano playing his profession and earns his livelihood from it; it may rather be the one who appears to be doing it "by the way."[1]

To the same extent that it surely is not everyone's calling to intensify his involvement with art to such a degree that he is willing to stand in the composer's shadow while re-"creating" in the best sense of the word, to that same extent, I claim, performances have always taken a shape that has nothing to do with a true reproduction. Because what ought to be known in order to perform a sonata by Beethoven is not known, the musical world found it easy to assign a role to reproduction in music that is in appalling contrast to its real origins. Undoubtedly, a misconception of the significance of performance in music and uncertainty about how to guarantee a true rendition have led to that proliferation of performances which is one of the causes of the decline of our art.

One might object that only a connoisseur requires a perfect performance and that for the audience at large an inferior one might do. I say "No!," for precisely the general public is most in need of an authentic and perceptive rendition in order to be led to the work; the knowledgeable listener can amply supplement shortcomings of the performer through his own imagination. The general public will simply accept a composition on faith; it is easier to doubt the quality of the composition than to suppose that the performer might have totally misrepresented it.

TWO

Mode of Notation and Performance

WHAT MUST BE REGARDED as the most fateful error in the performance of a musical work of art is the general view on the meaning of a composer's mode of notation. That which is decreed in the notation is considered the unalterable will of the composer, to be interpreted literally. Already the mere fact that our notation hardly represents more than neumes should lead the performer to search for the meaning behind the symbols. This is neglected, largely because of the difficulty of understanding the composer's intentions. If one were in the happy position of reaching this goal, however, one would realize that the author's mode of notation does not indicate his directions for the performance but, in a far more profound sense, represents the effect he wishes to attain. These are two separate things.[1]

Let us suppose the composer writes a sequence of half notes with marcato signs. This does not at all show the way the sequence should be played but indicates the effect the composer desires—leaving it up to the performer to find the means. In this particular case the pianist would have to sacrifice adhering precisely to the printed text, namely holding the half notes their full value; for the sake of a marcato effect he must reduce the length of each note, precisely in order to produce the marcato. From this example alone one can deduce that the mode of notation can be understood only from the point of view of the desired effect. A literal interpretation robs one of the very means leading to that effect.

The effect certainly must be completely at one with the execution. Whatever one has done—added to or taken away from the written note values—the final result, returning to our example, must give the impression of actual half notes. Herein lies the true secret of the art of performance: to find those peculiar ways of dissembling through which—via the detour of the effect—the mode of notation is realized.

In what follows we shall see that such ways exist; to discuss them all, however, would be impossible. Anyone who comes to understand the secrets of the mode of notation and of those as yet unrecognized means of dissembling, at last will also realize that our great masters were as inspired in their notation as they were in the actual composing. I should almost like to say that there is more to be admired in the notation than in the composition itself. What a pity that many editors misunderstand this, and simply do away with the composer's mode of notation! Substituting an entirely different one clearly leads to an entirely different result.

Just how far-reaching a relatively harmless (one might suppose) change in the mode of notation is can be seen in the general use of the double bar in newer editions. The manuscripts of the great masters up to Chopin do not show double bars before a change of key; the masters' writing continued without break, and the changed signature came after a single bar line. The typesetters' irritating custom of substituting a double bar for a single bar has the result that the eye receives the impression of a new beginning. Inevitably the performance must suffer from this. (The double bar in m. 84 of the first movement of Beethoven's Sonata for Piano and Cello op. 102, no. 2, is an example: this measure is interpreted and played as if it were the beginning of the recapitulation, which actually only occurs six measures later.)

One can already see from this example how urgent the need for an authentic text is: a text based on manuscripts and first editions, read not only in a philologically, diplomatically accurate manner but also musically. By the exact realization of the masters' clearly felt and considered mode of notation one can then achieve a plasticity of performance that virtually allows the piece to appear bodily, in light and shade.

In a final sense, however, all performance comes from within, not from the outside. The pieces breathe through their own lungs; they carry their own bloodstream—even without being labeled with concepts and names, as laymen would like, who demand: "Where is it written?"

THREE

The Technique of Playing the Piano

AT ALL TIMES THE NATURE of the piano, more than any other instrument such as violin or voice, has been misunderstood. The causes of this misunderstanding are the following:

1. Inadequate knowledge of the laws of composition by pianists, who are thereby prevented from expressing the composition's true content.
2. The nature of writing for the piano [i.e., multivoiced], which indeed gives pianists a harder task than either violinists or singers encounter in their single-voice writing.

One has to consider that piano texture frequently includes orchestral elements; to master its melodic and harmonic demands far more skills are necessary than for the purely horizontal line of a violin or voice part.

True understanding of the piano would have demanded of the player that he remain in the proximity of string instruments and the voice as well as of the orchestra. The difficulty inherent in this approach, however, caused pianists to make up for what they lacked, compensating for an inability by a manner of playing that was presented as a new, special piano style. The catchphrase "pianistic music" was invented to indicate an entire, separate region of music literature. There followed the development of a special "pianistic technique," which carefully avoided anything that might turn the piano into as expressive an instrument as the violin or the voice. Precisely here the fundamental difference between the great masters of composition on the one hand and the pure "virtuosos" on the other became apparent: the former used a piano technique that was identical to all other instruments' regarding expressiveness.[1]

In the following I shall describe various technical means whose use produces effects as we know them from singer and instrumentalist as well as from orchestral sound.

Piano Singing

[*This term, coined by Schenker, refers to applying principles of the voice and string instruments to the piano.*]

Piano singing is the stroking of the air through up-and-down motions of the hand—as the bow strokes the string:

$$\text{pressure} \quad \downarrow - \uparrow \quad \text{reflex.}$$

EXECUTION:

1. Depress key with pressure. The key is not to be touched thoughtlessly; the hand must drop appropriately as required by the "light-point." [By this term, Schenker refers to notes that require special emphasis. For a detailed explanation see chapter 8, "Dynamics," particularly sections "Freely Executed Shadings within *piano* and *forte*," and "Rhetorical Accents."]
2. Short reflex (Examples 3.1 and 3.2)
   Longer reflex—release gradually (Example 3.3).

A specific detail demands a *single* thrusting of the hand. This must be prepared from the outset, like bow strokes on strings and breathing in playing wind instruments; it must not be attempted during a passage while moving, from tone to tone as it were. The hand senses *in advance*, parallel to the composer's thinking ahead; it forms its gestures accordingly. Thus the meaning of the phrase determines the position and motion of the hands (Example 3.4). The sixteenths of m. 55 are not to be attacked in the last instant but prepared in advance. Compare also Example 10.1: here the violinist continues the bow stroke through the air. But the pianist, too, can produce this effect: he lifts his hand and lets it fly to the eighth note, continuing a single impulse.

Example 3.1 Beethoven, Sonata op. 53, I, mm. 3–4

Example 3.2 Chopin, Waltz op. 64, no.2, m. 33ff.

etc.

Example 3.3 Beethoven, Sonata op. 13, II, mm. 66–67

Example 3.4 Chopin, Berceuse op. 57, mm. 54–55

The hand may not lie; it must conform to the meaning of the voice-leading. It lies if in Example 3.5 this is violated by playing a^2–a^1; the connection must be f♯^{2} and c♯^{2}.

Certain painting gestures also belong among the necessary hand motions—now to the right, now to the left—in order to separate motives (Examples 3.6, 3.7, and 3.8).

Example 3.5 Mozart, Sonata K. 331, I, Theme, mm. 17–18 (see
Plate 2)

Example 3.6 Chopin, Mazurka op. 30, no. 1, mm. 29–32

Example 3.7 Chopin, Mazurka op. 24, no. 2, mm. 57–60

Example 3.8 Brahms, Waltz op. 39, no. 3, mm. 1–6 (see Plate 2)

Proximity of the Piano to the Orchestra

Pedal

No matter how much has been written and taught about this special
mechanism of the piano, its true nature has remained concealed.
One can best understand it by comparing the piano with the orchestra. Since the piano cannot provide all sustaining voices as the orchestra can, pedal gives it the possibility of compensating for these
missing parts. The damper pedal unshackles the overtones, whose
radiance substitutes for the orchestra's sustaining voices.

APPLICATION:

1. By connection of chords over and above additions and gaps,
   thanks to the resonance, a hiatus is avoided (Examples 3.9
   and 3.10).
2. Separation of chords by releasing the pedal creates shadows,
   thereby helping to define entities (Example 3.11).

Example 3.9 Beethoven, Sonata op. 13, I, mm. 49–50 (see Plate 2)

Example 3.10 Chopin, Waltz op. 42, mm. 221–29

Example 3.11 Brahms, Intermezzo op. 117, no. 1, mm. 1–2, m. 21

3. Beethoven assigns a particularly difficult role to the pedal in his Sonata op. 31, no. 2, I, mm. 143–48 and 153–59: one single pedal (poetically exceeding the limits of the instrument), the intimation of a voice, a message from above, in a dissonant register. (see Plate 2.)[2] See also Examples 3.12 and 3.13, where only pedal can effect the coupling of identical notes in the same register over some distance.

4. Because of the pedal's role of substituting for the filling voices in orchestral texture, it is rather risky to use it too much in accompanying woodwinds: this would double the sustaining voices. Here the pianist is well-advised to use the pedal sparingly. String instruments, however, less equipped for sustaining than for diminution,[3] are more compatible with the piano's pedal effect.

Hand Pedal

The path of the diminutions often is identical to that of orchestral sustaining voices. It is peculiar to the piano that it can let the diminutions prevail while the orchestral characteristics recede into the background. Of course this has the drawback that a player without imag-

Example 3.12 Beethoven, Sonata op. 31, no. 2, II, mm. 98–103

Example 3.13 Haydn, Sonata Hob. XVI: 52, II, mm. 51–54

ination will be unable to find ways of bringing out the hidden riches. In the case of Example 3.14a, a complete setting might look like Example 3.14b, perhaps played by horns and bassoons. The pianist must let this implied realization sound through the figure of the two bars. Only by holding the keys down, thus letting the chords be formed, is this possible. I suggest calling this manner of playing, which produces a pedal effect through the hand alone, *hand pedal*. It is a form, a substitute for legatissimo, a subtle augmentation of sound; it is not an obbligato voice! (See Examples 3.15 and 3.16.) Compare Beethoven Sonata op. 106, I, mm. 47–63: the tones are sustained by means of hand pedal, as in a French-horn setting (Example 3.17).

Air Pedal [Luftpedal]

Woodwinds, singers, and strings allow their breath or bow strokes to fade out when not specifically heeding a composer's direction to end a sound abruptly. This natural fading out continues through the air in space, regardless of meter or rhythm. The tone, as it were, "overflows" the limit of the actual note value. The notation is not thereby disregarded; it, too, is preserved. This phenomenon, quite natural to singers and woodwind and string players, is still entirely unknown to the pianist. The possibility of shading the tone by means of hand movements that produce this kind of fading out—C. P. E. Bach (*Essay on the True Art of Playing Keyboard Instruments* [hereafter *Essay*],

Example 3.14 Chopin, Nocturne op. 15, no. 2, mm. 1–2

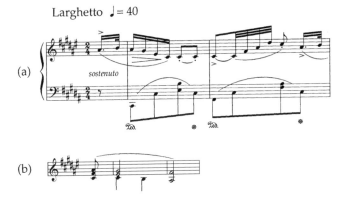

Example 3.15 Chopin, Sonata op. 58, III, mm. 1–2

Example 3.16 Chopin, Nocturne op. 27, no. 2, m. 1

Example 3.17 Beethoven, Sonata op. 106, I, mm. 47–48ff.

chap. 3, §18) calls it "Ziehen" [slurring]—is foreign to him. Whether one is playing in a slow or fast tempo, it is always possible to let even the shortest note—a thirty-second, a sixty-fourth—fade away. The shortest possible touch is sufficient to produce this effect. One might call it air pedal. When earlier composers asked for greater intensity on passing tones and dissonances, when, for instance, Beethoven always insisted (according to Schindler) that all neighboring notes should be emphasized in this way, the basis for this was the rule that light and shadow are necessary in instrumental music, comparable to the natural fading out of voice or woodwind instrument.(See Examples 3.18 and 3.19.) Compare also Haydn, Fantasia in C Major, Hob. XVII:4, m. 192: "tenuto intanto, finché non si sente più il suono"—until the sound has died out!

Dynamic Separation of Individual Fingers

In order to produce the character of polyphony it frequently is necessary to have different dynamics in different fingers—especially 5 of the left hand and 1 and 5 of the right—in this way, different orchestral instruments are suggested (Examples 3.20 and 3.21). When voices move in sixths or thirds a special effect occurs, much like an instrumental conversation.

Under certain circumstances, inner voices should be brought out instead of the melody, as for instance in Example 3.22; otherwise the interaction becomes incomprehensible.

Basses that occur after the beats should usually be played louder than the melody; the special attraction of this technique will otherwise go unnoticed (Example 3.23). Orchestral thinking also influences the splitting of a single chord (Example 3.24).

Octaves

In this context, the playing of octaves must be given particular attention. The two fingers never should be played with the same strength; depending on the register, either 1 or 5 has to lead. In Example 3.25, the higher octave is the leading one. In Example 3.26, on the contrary, the lower octave should always lead.

When the bass moves in octaves, the result often is a certain orchestral interaction of registers, as if the lower note were played by the basses and the higher one by the cellos. Compare Example 3.27; in this case, the lower voice should be brought out.

Rendition of the Bass

The most effective contribution to a beautiful performance is an appropriately played bass; precisely that is rarely heard. Lacking full awareness of the harmonic and contrapuntal relationships, the pianist tends to neglect the left hand, which generally shows these ele-

Example 3.18 Beethoven, Sonata op. 27, no. 1, I, mm. 79–81 (for explanation of arrows, see p. 54)

Example 3.19 Beethoven, Sonata op. 90, II, mm. 209–11

Example 3.20 Chopin, Prelude op. 28, no. 6, mm. 1–2 (see Plate 4)

Example 3.21 Brahms, Variations on a Theme by Paganini, op. 35, var. VI, mm. 1–2 (see Plate 4)

Example 3.22 Beethoven, *Eroica* Variations, op. 35, "A quattro," mm. 1–2

Example 3.23 Beethoven, Sonata op. 57, II, mm. 17–20ff.

Example 3.24 Chopin, Ballade op. 23, mm. 8–10, similar to m. 22 l.h.

Example 3.25 Mozart, Sonata K. 331, I, var. 3, m. 17

Example 3.26 Beethoven, Sonata op. 106, III, mm. 22–23

Example 3.27 Mozart, Sonata K. 331, II, mm. 1–2

ments most clearly, in favor of the right, which usually leads melodi-
cally. Thereby precisely that element is omitted which brings the
piano close to the orchestra. The performer must understand that the
bass of the piano should receive as varied a treatment of dynamic nuances as the bass line of the orchestra, which has to follow its own
specially described shadings. Conductors cannot be spared the criti-
cism that, like bad pianists, they tend to favor the high register over
the low. Thereby they deprive themselves of the most grandiose
effects—effects brought about by a nuanced, carefully shaped bass.

Example 3.28 Chopin, Etude op. 25, no. 1, m. 1ff.

For all these reasons the pianist would be well-advised to pay the greatest attention to the left hand. In this context, I should like to point out a unique example (Example 3.28). When one studies the original notation of this piece one notices that Chopin writes both large- and small-sized notes, reserving the large not only for the melody but for individual bass notes as well. Looking more closely at the notation of the bass, one sees that among several identical bass notes, only one is emphasized by the large size while the rest are small. This particular mode of notation—how inspired, and what a pity that other composers did not use it as well!—shows clearly that even the fundamental tones of the bass should be played with varied nuances.

May this example stimulate the pianist to pursue the question of shaping the bass line, thereby preventing the bad effect of a monotonously played bass. He should not wait for the instant a cantabile line is taken over by the left hand—to bring this out is nothing special in itself—but even in those places where the basses are only supporting or passing they should be shaped in the most careful manner.

FOUR

Non Legato

EXPLAINING THE NATURE OF non legato, particularly to the pianist, is not easy. An example from the orchestral literature may enlighten him. He may observe how Brahms handles the instrumentation of the fugue in the third movement of his *German Requiem*: the strings do not play legato, whereas the woodwinds, in executing the same motives simultaneously, play legato. The combination of these two is what I recommend to pianists as a model for a non legato effect. That which the strings imply, namely separate bow strokes (i.e., pressure) on each note, must become part of the final effect as much as the legato of the woodwinds. In other words: without being executed as a full legato, each note must nevertheless carry the pressure of its own weight.

Comparison to violin technique brings further material for instructive distinctions. It is common knowledge that the violin's sound depends on the length of the bow strokes used. The art of performing, of expressing sound-ideas, lies in alternating long and short bow strokes and in using an abundance of nuances. The same holds true for the "bowing technique" of the pianist's hand. Pianists, too, can and should make use of the longer and shorter "bows" the violinist uses. The identity of the two techniques is such that the pianist's technique includes the imitation of a suddenly broken-off bow stroke. The violinist must assure utmost precision in stopping the bow, as keeping it in contact with the string longer would prolong the sound beyond the desired limit. Likewise, in non legato the pianist has strictly to define the limit of the sound's duration. The correct execution will be ensured by a sudden jolt that leads from the key to the lower arm and the elbow. Lacking such a specific termination of the sound, the pianist will fail to give the composer an effect not withheld by either violinist or singer.

If we consider the history of musical technique, it becomes clear that non legato must have been all the more prevalent in earlier epochs when phrases generally lacked synthesis; that is, they were short and undifferentiated. [Translator's note: "synthesis" is Schenker's term for his concept of organic unity, i.e., the idea of a work of art in which every part is organically related, supported by a single unifying background structure. See quote from O. Jonas in Editor's Introduction, p. xii.] Larger motivic units that give the opportunity for contrasting groups of connected notes and of separate ones did not exist. The contrapuntal treatment used in oldest times shows that nearly all notes merely serving as contrapuntal parts had equal aesthetic significance and equal function. Only later, with increasingly rich tonal content, did differentiation of notes appear, here joined in groups, there separated. Eventually that true legato developed which guaranteed the unity of a group of notes by using a single breath or bow stroke.

The increasing use of legato simultaneously with increasing content can be appreciated most clearly in Beethoven, whose contemporaries admired his legato playing above all. Neither his way of composing nor his playing would have created the sensation it did had he not introduced to a high degree that especially beautiful legato which could not have been composed or played heretofore. From this it can be concluded that the works of the masters who preceded Beethoven, particularly those of J. S. Bach, are more appropriately performed in non legato than in legato.

FIVE

Legato

IN CONTRAST TO NON LEGATO, legato always represents a specific act of will, aimed at connecting small and smallest units [i.e., groups of notes]. C. P. E. Bach's choice of words (*Essay*, chap. 3, §18) indicates this fact: "schleifen," "ziehen" [to slur, to slide]—these expressions certainly indicate a specific intention. Pressure and legato must be willed; lack of pressure and non legato are largely appropriate where the demands of synthesis and diminution do not require pressure and legato.

Legato technique is by far the most difficult and complicated manner of playing for the pianist. Just as the violinist is enabled to connect several notes by a continuous bow stroke on one string, as the singer can connect several notes with one breath, similarly a quiet hand position is the only one that gives the possibility of playing several notes in succession so that they—melting into one another, as it were—form a chain of notes with the same effect as a legato group on the violin or in singing.

Held Notes

Even more than on a quiet hand, legato depends on a special technique, which Example 5.1 will clarify. The sequence of notes at (a) is known as an independent phenomenon by the term "portamento."[1] In order to attain the desired expression, the pianist must continue holding the first note even after the d^2 has been played—best if ar-

Example 5.1 Beethoven, Sonata op. 57, I, m. 3

ticulated as in (b). Keeping one finger down while another key has already been struck assures the effect of a slide most readily. This same technique can also be used for a larger sequence of notes regardless of dissonances.

The pianist thus has a device, heretofore unrecognized, for giving the piano similarity to the orchestra: by holding down a key even without the composer's indication, that tone is raised to the rank of a true sustaining note, as in Example 5.2. At times the composer indicates this effect by specifically requiring held notes (Examples 5.3, 5.4, and 5.5). In such cases, it would be an error to assume that the written-out sustaining voices mean more than just that; it would therefore be wrong to emphasize them—just as it would be inappropriate for the orchestral instruments to do so, were the piece arranged for orchestra.

By using the holding-down technique for a series of notes, a new voice can be generated on the piano that exceeds the character of a sustaining voice and becomes obbligato. If in Example 5.6 the fingers are held somewhat longer than written, an obbligato voice appears that undoubtedly would be expressed by a different instrument in the orchestra. When larger leaps make it impossible to hold the fingers down, the impression of an obbligato voice must be created by varied gradations of touch[2] (Example 5.7).

In some instances, it proves to be appropriate in a longer series of notes to hold some fingers down longer than written (Example 5.8). The purpose of this way of playing is not so much the connection of adjacent notes in the sense of a simple legato nor that of producing a sustaining voice, but rather that of ensuring a quiet and steady hand appropriate to a longer sequence of notes. It then appears as if the held fingers protectively foster the equal touch of the remaining fingers.

The note to be held is not always chosen according to harmonic or motivic principles—certainly the most plausible reason—for often the just-described procedure takes place only as a purely technical device. (See Example 7.4.)

Example 5.2 (a) C. P. E. Bach, *Essay on the True Art of Playing Keyboard Instruments,* chap. 3, §18, fig. 168; (b) Beethoven, Piano Quintet (also published as Piano Quartet), op. 16, I, mm. 22–23

(a)

(b)

Example 5.3 J. S. Bach, English Suite no. 3, Sarabande, mm. 17–20

Example 5.4 J. S. Bach, English Suite no. 2, Prelude, mm. 23–25

Example 5.5 Chopin, Nocturne op. 62, no. 1, mm. 4–9

Example 5.6 Handel, Suite no. 1, Aria con variazioni, var. 1, m.1
(a) and (b)

(a)

(b)

Example 5.7 Chopin, Ballade op. 47, mm. 116–119

Example 5.8 Chopin, Etude op. 10, no. 12, mm. 73–74

Articulating Legato

The identity of legato technique in violin, voice, and piano can be
observed in a particular type of legato. This consists of individual
notes within a group that receive pressure separately, notwithstanding a strictly observed legato. The violinist can finger individual notes
while continuing to draw his bow in undulating motions without
compromising the legato. The singer, similarly, is able to emphasize
individual notes within one single breath. The same effect can be at-

Example 5.9 Beethoven, Sonata op. 7, III (a) mm. 1–3, (b) mm. 25–28

tained by the pianist if he plays legato as described previously with strictly held keys, simultaneously moving the arm and hand in an elastic, swaying motion in order to play the following key from a higher point than he would otherwise. Perhaps a different image describes this technique more suitably: it is as if the arm were striding back and forth in the keys, which serve as its firm ground.

The type of legato to be used depends on the place in the music in question, of course. Thus it is the desired expression that finally decides if further nuances of the two main kinds of legato are to be used. Under certain circumstances—when appropriate—the hand that is to play legato must become quiet to the point of rigidity. Analogously, an actor's voice in a similar case would remain on one pitch in order to express great tension in a given situation. But how many nuances lie between rigidity and a relaxed, seemingly flowing quiet! The other type of expressive legato, by contrast, permits countless nuances that result from the arm's being alternately raised and lowered while moving up and down the keys. With each change—the effect should not be underestimated!—its own particular expression is achieved. Compare the two situations shown in Example 5.9.

Ways of Dissembling

At times certain ways of dissembling can help to give an impression of legato even where, strictly speaking, legato is impossible. Thus a legato effect is attained in Chopin's Etude op. 25, no. 8, by means of gliding elbows. Here, in quickest tempo, the gesture stands for the effect. The same means is to be used in Brahms, Variations on a

Theme by Handel, op. 24, var. 6. Likewise, dissembling of a lower order includes the legato of double notes or chords. In such cases, it is entirely sufficient to use a legato fingering in the upper or, where appropriate, lower voice of the interval in question. At any rate, this "one-sided" legato will simulate legato in all voices, benefiting also those notes that were not played legato.

Where it is impossible to use such a one-sided fingering, a mere gesture of the hand can substitute for a true legato. In this succession of tones, for instance,

the hand must "dig into" the D, from there moving on to f♯ with a faint motion; the held-over sound thus provides the legato. (See Plate 4.)

In Example 5.10, the left hand takes over the sixteenth c, holds it as a whole note through the measure, and thus assures legato to the next measure's chord. Chopin himself gives us an interesting example (Example 5.11). Here the original fingering 1–1–1 produces an impression of held notes without further indications by the composer. Obviously resting on the fourth finger (c^2), the hand easily takes in stride the notes played by the thumb.

For the same reason I recommend playing a section from Mendelssohn's "Spring Song" as in Example 5.12, where holding the notes is that medium for the illusion which leads to a legato effect even though the fingering appears to produce the opposite effect. Similarly Example 5.13, where through a change of fingers the held a♭ enables the melody to produce the effect of a portamento from $a\flat^2$ to $b\flat^1$, also Example 5.14, giving a portamento effect $c\sharp^1$ to $b\flat^2$. Note that the effect of portamento, imitating that of a singer or violinist, is not limited to the performer but inevitably is transmitted to the listener.

From all this the conclusion should be drawn that the impression of legato can be created even without actual legato playing inasmuch as the possibility of appropriate ways of dissembling exists.

Change of Finger on the Same Key

An eminent aid in producing a true legato is changing the finger on the same key. See Schumann's comment on Caprice III of the *Concert Studies on Caprices by Paganini:* "The editor . . . points out the silent changing of fingers on one key, which often creates a most beautiful effect in an Adagio . . ." (Example 5.15).

Example 5.10 Chopin, Etude op. 10, no. 8, mm. 13–14

Example 5.11 Chopin, *Three Etudes*, no. 1, mm. 46–47

 Example 5.12 Mendelssohn, *Songs without Words,* op. 62, no. 6 ("Spring Song"), mm. 19–23

Example 5.13 Chopin, Waltz op. 42, mm. 244–246

Example 5.14 Beethoven, Rondo op. 51, no. 2, m. 39

Example 5.15 Schumann, Caprice III of the Concert Studies on
Caprices by Paganini

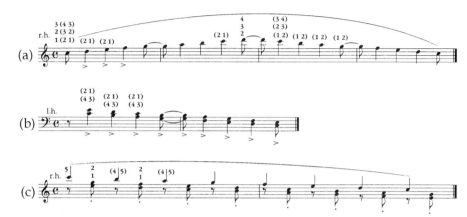

Such a change of finger in itself gives an impression similar to the
sound transmitted by a singer or violinist. Just as the singer and the
violinist continue, enlivening the sound with, respectively, a spun-
out breath or a bow stroke, the pianist gives an illusion of spinning
the sound on by changing fingers on one note. The quick changing
of fingers approximates a continuous presence; without finger
change, played only *once*, the sound appears fixed.

The most perfect legato effect, however, comes from the continuing dragging along of one finger, for example

$$5\text{-}\overgroup{4, 5}\text{-}\overgroup{4, 5}\text{-}4 \quad \text{or} \quad 4\text{-}\overgroup{3, 4}\text{-}\overgroup{3, 4}\text{-}3 \,,$$

creating the effect of a series of tones executed only by the fifth or
fourth finger. This way a special kind of unity develops through the
fingering that resembles a *single* breath or bow stroke. Such a finger
technique allows the tones to flow into one another with an inti-
macy unequaled by any other legato technique. (Example 5.16).

Legato of Identical Notes

In spite of their similar appearance, a distinction must be made between the previous Examples and a case such as Example 5.17: the
context proves that Beethoven's way of writing

Example 5.16 Beethoven, Sonata op. 110, III, m. 5

Example 5.17 Beethoven, Symphony no. 3, op. 55, II, mm. 217–18

on the downbeat of m. 218 in Example 5.17 does not mean merely

 ;

rather, both sixteenths that follow the bar line must be articulated in the strictest legatissimo. In Example 5.18, too, the first two b^2s are tied; nevertheless, both must be played. When Beethoven writes as in Example 5.19 (a), a different effect is created than in (b), which should rather be played as in (c). Beethoven's notation stands for a kind of *portato* (d), but with the difference that the strings do not play the three notes with one bow stroke, raising the bow after each note, but change the bow thus: ⊓ V ⊓ .

It was Beethoven who introduced this kind of *portato* with bow changes. Also see Example 5.20, in expression to be played like

but with a change of bow.

Example 5.18 Chopin, Mazurka op. 17, no. 2, m. 4

Example 5.19 Beethoven, String Quartet op. 59, no. 2, I, m. 59

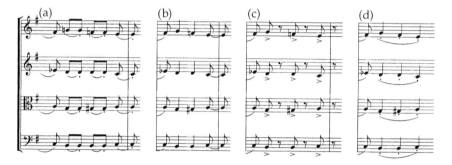

Example 5.20 Beethoven, String Quartet op. 74, II, m. 30

SIX

Staccato

FAR FROM BOTH LEGATO AND NON LEGATO, staccato technique
serves the pianist—as it does singer and violinist—to shorten the individual tone considerably. The prerequisite for this of course is the
condition that initially the single tone was meant to receive particular pressure. In this case, however, even more than abbreviation itself, the height to which the hand is raised or thrust after cutting
short the tone in order to drop on the next key must be considered.
In other words: also in staccato a certain distance from the key is related to a different expression. One has to observe furthermore that
the height has a crucial effect for two reasons: not only is the elasticity of rebounding from the key thereby expressed, but the strength
of the attack of the following key is determined simultaneously.
Thus the height must represent a specific point above the keys.

Under certain circumstances, particularly when a crescendo or
decrescendo is combined with this (as in Example 6.1), the pianist,

Example 6.1 Mozart, Sonata K. 331, I, var. 5, m. 10

like the violinist, who can make a transition from longer to shorter
bow strokes (or vice versa), can create a series of highlights which—
as the following figure shows—can run in a gradual scale from high
to low or from low to high

SEVEN

Fingering

IF ONE CONSIDERS THAT THE polyphonic composing of a J. S. Bach demanded all possible freedom in fingering, and that the freedom in the masterworks of our Classical composers encouraged unfettered fingering as well, then it is hardly understandable that our generation could delude itself into believing that it is behaving more freely and progressively in regard to fingering than the Classical masters. Quite apart from the fact that it was the creation of their works that gave rise to the art of fingering in the first place (for which reason alone they may be considered superior to performers), and quite apart from the fact that they frequently left documents of their art of fingering, one must specifically stress that the content of their work was always created according to the needs of synthesis, never merely according to those of the hand.[1] From this alone it follows that fingerings in their works, given the nature of the content, must be more difficult than those in later works, which often merely arose from the hand.

Only once, namely in Chopin, did the needs of his own, particular synthesis and those of the hand fuse so perfectly that synthesis never was sacrificed to the hand, or vice versa. Now considering that even Chopin's genius shows considerably reduced potency compared to that of our great masters, one should not be astonished that the compositions of all other composers, least of all excepting Liszt, offer no more opportunities for beautiful fingerings, as here the composition itself, as it were, spoils fingering [but see Schenker's

remarks on Brahms's piano style, p.72]. This may explain why, for instance, Joachim did not like to play or, rather, never could decide to
play Dvořák's chamber music: regardless of all the qualities that
raised it far above the entire contemporary output, at the same time
it offered him no opportunities for that highest art of bow technique
which he had to use in the performance of the Classical quartet.

Freedom of fingering, as we admire it in the earliest piano methods (before Czerny), was as much a product of the general non
legato technique as of expression. All the subtle fingering skills—far
from the usual scale fingerings 1–2–3–1–2–3–4 and 1–2–3–4–
1–2–3—were possible only within the context of non legato technique, which by its very nature can be quite well served by a certain
degree of nonchalance.

Later developments such as chordal writing, multivoiced spread-
out reaches, specifically indicated legato (which often because of the
many voices cannot be carried out strictly), and pedal technique
force us to use similarly free fingering today. Similar freedom, different cause. The free mobility of the "soul" of a work of art ever will
demand total freedom of fingering.

The normal hand position, *centralizing* the fingers 1–5, is always
the point of departure. Any other position is always "impromptu
fingering." Larger reaches—the *spreading out* of the fingers—must be
based on the synthesis or at least on a technical need. In Example 7.1,
$c\sharp^2$ must be released the instant $c\sharp^3$ is played; the thumb rejoins the
other fingers, virtually in the span of a fifth, just as indicated by the
content, which moves from $c\sharp^3$ to $f\sharp^2$. In Example 7.2, it would be
impossible to play $c\flat^4$–$b\flat^3$–$a\flat^3$ on the second beat with sufficient emphasis were one to keep the hand streched out to the octave $c\flat^3$–$c\flat^4$
or to a diminished seventh d^3–$c\flat^4$. Under no circumstances should
the lower fingering be used. Even with the upper one, the thumb
must release the position of the d^3 immediately, as the hand must
contract to join the fifth finger on $c\flat^4$.[2]

Fingering also must be honest; the hand—like the mouth—must
speak the truth; it must correspond to the voice-leading (Example 7.3).

In Example 7.4, too, in spite of the slur, the fingering changes according to the change of the chord. See the original fingerings of the
masters in manuscripts and first editions![3]

Long, short, and mixed fingerings should be used in runs, thirds,
sixths, and arpeggios, depending on the chord—on its meaning in
the sense of the synthesis.[4] Long, for example, in Example 7.5, but

Example 7.1 Mozart, Piano Concerto K. 488, II, m. 93ff.

Example 7.2 Beethoven, Sonata op. 57, I, m. 60

Example 7.3 J. S. Bach, French Suite in E Major, Allemande m 20. The role played by the sixteenth as head-tone of a motive is more important than its function as ending of the accompanying bass line. Only the fingering 5 | 5 can separate the two.

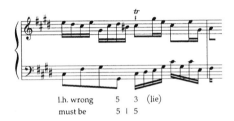

Example 7.4 Brahms, Intermezzo op. 118, no. 1, mm. 14–15

Example 7.5 Mozart, Rondo K. 511, m. 147

Example 7.6 C. P. E. Bach, *Probesonate* no. 4, I, m. 9, original fingering

Example 7.7 C. P. E. Bach, *Probesonate* no. 4, I, m. 16 original fingering. (1–2 for the neighboring–note motion around b, but 4–4–4 quasi motivic.)

short in Example 7.6, which closes a section of the movement. Similarly in Example 7.7.

Often the masters specifically asked for one special free kind of fingering: the sliding finger. (Examples 7.8, 7.9, and 7.10 are original fingerings.) See also Example 5.11.

Sliding fingers in the service of the synthesis are also required in the case of Example 7.11. The technical need for sliding thumbs in lower voices of third, sixth, and octave passages as well as in chord progressions can equally serve to produce the most intense expressiveness, as, for instance, in Example 7.12. The fingering follows the upper line, that is, the melodic line. In both relevant segments:

it uses 3–4–5 on the first three tones. The greatest advantage of this is that also beyond these segments the third finger falls on a black key

Example 7.8 C. P. E. Bach, *Probesonate*, no. 6, Fantasia

Example 7.9 Beethoven, *Diabelli* Variations, op. 120, var. 8, mm. 17
and 24

Example 7.10 Chopin, Sonata op. 58, I, mm. 11 and 147

Example 7.11 Chopin, Nocturne op. 9, no. 3, mm. 19–20;
six notes, five fingers!

Example 7.12 Chopin, Etude op. 25, no. 6, mm. 5–6

Example 7.13 Liszt, *Soirées de Vienne*, 6, 2d ed., mm. 291, 430, and 297

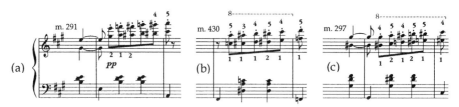

and the fourth on a white. The price paid for this advantage is a rather minor one, namely that the two half steps in the lower voice that consist of two successive white keys must be played by 1-1.

It is always the required expression that must decide if the fingering in the case of thirds should follow the upper or lower line or a combination of the two. This also holds true for sixths (Example 7.13); one uses a fingering that follows either the lower chromatic line as far as possible, as in (a); or the upper one, as in (b); or a combination, as in (c).

EIGHT

Dynamics

piano and *forte* as Basic Conditions

It is mistaken to consider the dynamic concepts *piano* and *forte* only in one single sense as weak and strong, as if an absolute and measurable quality of sound were meant by them. Rather, two entirely different meanings are possible: at times, *piano* and *forte* indeed are expressions of *quantity* in a purely physical sense, comparable to a large number of parts in the orchestra (thus, f in a particular place in the piano work corresponds to an orchestral *forte* with full, resounding instrumentation while p corresponds to a more modest instrumentation); at other times, however, they have a meaning that is, unfortunately, always overlooked. This meaning, going well beyond quantity, refers to a psychological *quality* of great elasticity and relativity: thus occasionally *forte* can be interpreted as having emotional resonance and *piano* as being less the low point of a physical quantity than an intimate utterance.[1]

From this double meaning it follows that only the content of the composition can decide which of the two is appropriate. Thus all *fortes* are no more alike than all *pianos*. Merely understood quantitatively, the directive p in Example 8.1 would lead to a wrong interpretation. There is no doubt that the second theme, by its very nature cantabile and espressivo, must be played with intense, intimate expressiveness, coming as it does after the figurations of the modulation section. If the pianist further considers that the strong sound

Example 8.1 Beethoven, Sonata op. 110, I, mm. 20–21

Example 8.2 Chopin, Polonaise op. 26, no. 1, Meno mosso mm. 1–4

of the preceding figurations as well as the high register in which the new motive appears would give a physically weak *piano* a yet weaker, paler appearance than would ordinarily be the case, then he must, for the sake of contrast and because of the high register, resort to playing the *piano* in this spot with strength (in an inner sense) and with a full sound. Another example: the middle section of the Polonaise in Example 8.2 contains the instruction "p con anima," which expresses the wish for an enthusiastically played, intense *piano*.

Pianissimo under certain circumstances means nothing other than stillness—that particular kind of stillness which does not lose its character even if one or more voices float through space. Thus it does not depend so much on dynamic weight but rather on the impression of stillness, through which an individual voice may yet sound penetratingly. Stillness, too, lets voices be heard clearly—in a certain sense even more clearly than does noise. Of course one has to be able to sense just when the composer is describing that kind of stillness. See Wagner, beginning and end of the Prelude to "Lohengrin."

The Rhapsody op. 79, no. 1, by Brahms can serve as an example of *forte* in the psychological sense. Observe that here *ff* only bursts out in two places (in mm. 60 and 64 and, similarly, mm. 188 and 192) and that most of the work takes place within *f*. From its mere length, then, it can be deduced that what is meant is less a *forte* in the physical sense (this would be unplayable or, if played, would lead to a monotonous, mindless show of strength) than a state of intense excitement that, as the construction of the work shows, generates the rhapsodic momentum.

Specifically Indicated Shadings within *piano* and *forte*

Only if the preceding characterizations of *piano* and *forte* have been fully assimilated can one understand the often ingenious, even in-spired indications of nuances by our masters, who similarly want *mf* or *mp*, like the basic dynamic levels themselves, understood now in the spiritual, now in the physical, sense, as appropriate.

To determine whether quantity of sound or quality of emotion is to be emphasized, *p cresc. f* must be examined. Far more interesting is the nuance *p cresc. p*. It would be worthwhile to trace it back his-torically in the works of the masters, as it definitely does not ante-date C. P. E. Bach. More than any other nuance it seems to attest to its origin in the emotions: a more or less passing intense agitation within a spiritually expressed *p*. The uses of these written-out nu-ances are manifold. One can hardly express them in a more subtly varied way than Beethoven does in his Sonata op. 109, I, Second theme, mm. 9–13:

$$f \ \textbf{\textit{p}} \ \textit{cresc.} \ \big| \ f \ \textbf{\textit{p}} \ \textit{cresc.} \ \big| \textbf{\textit{p}} \ \textit{cresc.} \text{------} \ \big| \ f \ \textbf{\textit{p}} \ \textit{cresc.} \quad \textbf{\textit{p}} \ \big| \ f$$

Far more than nuances within *piano*, those within *forte* suffer from being misunderstood; already the basic conception of *forte*, which unfortunately never is interpreted in any but the physical sense, is entirely erroneous. As a result performers have never been particu-larly inclined to acknowledge or to carry out shadings within *forte*—whether they are specifically indicated or not. And while to a degree performers have concerned themselves with shadings within *piano*, they interpret *forte* merely as a show of physical strength. Once they were guilty of this, it was inevitable that they should misunderstand even clearly marked nuances, just where these were at their most in-spired. One need only see the many, ever-recurring shadings *f cresc. f* in the Rhapsody op. 79, no. 1, by Brahms—virtually a hallmark of this composer!—which, similar to *p cresc. p* again mean agitation within a general *forte*. (See earlier discussion.)

Beethoven, Symphony no. 7, op. 92, IV, mm. 427–43:

$$\textbf{\textit{fff}} \ \text{-} \ \textbf{\textit{p}} \ \textit{cresc.} \ \text{-} \ \textbf{\textit{fff}}$$

Beethoven, String Quartet op. 18, no. 6, IV, mm. 29–34:

$$\textbf{\textit{p}} \ \big| \ \textbf{\textit{f p}} \ \big| \ \textbf{\textit{f p}} \ \big| \ \textbf{\textit{f p}} \ \big| \ \textbf{\textit{sf}} \ \big| \ \textbf{\textit{sf}} \ \big|$$

Haydn, *Creation*, no. 19, m. 27:

$$f \; (p \; \text{——} \; f)$$

(conceived as shadows within *forte* as well as descriptively:

$$\text{"}e \; \text{——} \; wig\text{"} \; [\text{eternal}])$$

Schubert, Sonata D. 894, III:

$$f\text{–}p \; (\; pp \;) \; :\|:f \; (\mathit{ff}) \; \text{–} \; pp \quad f$$

Brahms, Piano Concerto op. 15, I, mm. 1–25 (timpani).

Freely Executed Shadings within *piano* and *forte*

However, nuances are not always specifically indicated; more frequently they must be read between the lines, as it were. Here again
the curious fact emerges that the pianist uses shadings within *piano*
much more naturally than within *forte*; he should similarly force himself with strict self-discipline to carry out such subtle inflections
within *forte* as well.[2] Nuances of this kind are as thoroughly unde-
finable as the vibrations in the rise and fall of the voice of an orator or
actor and thus entirely defy a precise depiction. The attempt to add
such shadings to editions of older masterworks is a grave error of
certain editors. Once the performer sees them written out, the mere
optical reflex tempts him to such a degree that he will exaggerate the
nuance where, left to his own resources, he would surely be more re-
strained. After all, something must be left up to the performer!

It must be considered a counterreaction in our time that the works
of older composers are being restored precisely to their original
state after so many earlier distortions. However, a far greater unde-
sirable consequence occurs in the markings of modern works (i.e.,
in Strauss, Reger, Mahler, etc.). The manner in which these composers mark their works is so tortured, bursting with superfluous detail, that one senses their suspicion of the incompetence of their fel-
low musicians.

Example 8.3 Beethoven, *Egmont* Overture, op. 84, mm. 28–35

The following principle is thus valid: whether in *forte* or in *piano*, shadings are necessary, similar to the play of light and shade in legato and non legato. Even if not explicitly prescribed, they are part of the performance in a dissembling manner (Example 8.3).

Schubert, Symphony no. 9, D. 944, I, mm. 1–2:

also in *ff*, m. 40:

Sources of light connect regions of light—thus energy is saved, and understanding fostered: a *single* glance takes in the before and after. In contrast we have the clumsy plodding of relentlessly heavy playing. See also Beethoven, Sonata op. 106, I, mm. 112–21:

Also Beethoven, Sonata op. 111, I, mm. 146–52:

(*sf* with rests in the shade of the *ff*, increasing in density to *portato*, then to half notes, then to legato)

From these examples it can be seen that each unit requires light and shade but once: should two points of emphasis appear to occur in the same motive, this would only be understandable from the synthesis, as in Example 8.4. The g^1 of the second bar ought to be in the shade but nonetheless has an > above it, as it simultaneously is the beginning of something new.

forte–piano

How the directive *f–p* is to be understood depends entirely on the meaning of the composition. In older works, by J. S. Bach, Handel, and their predecessors for example, it often means a sudden alternation between *forte* and *piano*, based on the so-called echo effect. (See J. S. Bach Partita III for Violin Solo, Prelude; it is obvious that in a case like this any bridging by means of a *crescendo* or *diminuendo* is inappropriate.)

Example 8.4 Chopin, Mazurka op. 24, no. 1, mm. 1–4

In most cases, however, *f–p*, whether close together or more widely separated, can only be evaluated and executed by means of the emotions for underlying reasons integral to the composition. Thus, for example, Mozart's instruction in the Menuet of his String Quartet in G Major (Example 8.5) cannot be understood in the physical sense and performed accordingly, but rather in the sense of a notation of marcato signs >, ∧ , which were not yet in general use. The excerpt from C. P. E. Bach's Sonata in G Major is an ingenious example (Example 8.6). Similarly the markings *f* (or *sf*) and *p* that are barely separated call for that effect to which we aspire with ▭, again not in the sense of a sudden contrast (Example 8.7). The execution of Example 8.8 is difficult. Dropping from *forte* into *piano,* in other words into negative physical strength, one must invest the *piano* with those qualities it lacks in relation to the preceding *forte.* Suddenly more subdued, the intensity of emotion must attempt to replace the earlier *forte* while not exceeding *piano.* The *piano* summons inner forces to a kind of climax, thus apparently contradicting what—seen superficially—it actually asks for.

The way *forte* and *piano* can also color the individual sections of a phrase, particularly in older music (in C. P. E. Bach, for example), I have shown in my *Beitrag zur Ornamentik.*

The extraordinarily cogent technique of our older masters often brought with it different dynamics in each hand, as shown in Example 8.9. Thus for compositional reasons, editors as well as players who put uniform dynamics on the same beat are mistaken.

A curious example by C. P. E. Bach (Example 8.10) shows the two hands with opposite dynamics.

Example 8.5 Mozart, String Quartet K. 387, II, mm. 1–8

Example 8.6 C. P. E. Bach, *Sonatas for Connoisseurs and Amateurs, First Collection*, No. 6, II, m. 12

Example 8.7 Mozart, String Quintet K. 516, III, mm. 18–22

Example 8.8 Beethoven, String Quartet op. 130, I, mm. 15–16

Rhetorical Accents

Tension–relaxation = light–shade are as essential in music as in language, where they occur naturally in syllable and sentence construction. If our manner of speaking were continually to remain on one pitch and the syllables were the same length we would have no structure, no differentiation, and thus we would lose any possibility of communication. Therefore, a speaker gives each syllable, whether prefix or root syllable, a different emphasis. And only this contrast in strength, color, length creates differences, interrelationships, continuity—in other words, communication.

Example 8. 9 Mozart, Sonata K. 310, II, mm. 26–30

Example 8.10 C. P. E. Bach, *Sonatas for Connoisseurs and Amateurs, First Collection*, no. 6, I, mm. 52–53

In speech these conditions of light and shade are so familiar that they go unnoticed by speakers of the same language; in music, alas, we have not come so far. In singing, again, it is the syllables that preclude unshaded light. Those instrumentalists who come nearer to speech through breath or bow technique also possess a greater ability to differentiate light and shade than the pianist. The latter tends to touch the keys in an undifferentiated way only because they lie there in front of him; pressing them down is no trouble, and he is spared any association with speech. The performance inevitably must suffer from such a misguided conception.

Rhetorical accents refer to metric organization (for example, the upbeat), segments of form, and form as such. Only they can clarify the rhythm: without the contrast of rhetorical accents, special rhythm does not exist, no matter how strictly player or conductor adheres to the meter. The dotted rhythm in the first movement of Symphony no. 7, op. 92, by Beethoven can only be made understandable through the disposition of rhetorical accents; otherwise the rhythm would die in itself. The eloquent effect of emphasizing the weak beat in the second theme of the first movement of Symphony no. 9, op. 125, by Beethoven (mm. 80–83) is noteworthy:

compare this with the clumsiness of a more usual accentuation:

(See also Example 8.11.)

In the widest sense, the frequent emphasis on the middle of a figure also belongs among rhetorical effects:

(and not   )

(Examples 8.12, 8.13, and 8.14). It is noteworthy, however, that ⟨ ⟩ in Beethoven not infrequently means a momentary halting, not an actual ⟨ ⟩ in a dynamic sense.

Certain laws are generally valid. In principle the following are to be emphasized:

1. the head-tone of a motive >
2. a neighboring note

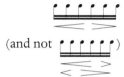

3. an accented passing note

4. a suspension

Re no. 1, Beethoven, Sonata for Piano and Violin op. 24, IV, mm. 1-2 (see Example 9.21). In spite of the repeated notes in m. 2, m. 1 has the main accent; the dotted half note in m. 3 is supported by the meter with no further emphasis. Similarly the opening of the fourth movement of Beethoven's Sonata op. 22 (Example 9.22).

Example 8.11 Chopin, Nocturne op. 37, no. 2, mm. 44–48

Example 8.12 Beethoven, String Quartet op. 18, no. 6, IV, mm. 77–78

Example 8.13 Beethoven, Sonata op. 106, III, m. 49

Example 8.14 Beethoven, Symphony no. 1, op. 21, II, mm. 35–39

Example 8.15 Chopin, Scherzo op. 54, mm. 460–66

Re no. 4: The dissonance always must be emphasized; the resolution always must be in the shade. Examples of resolutions of suspensions with $<$ find their special justification in the synthesis —usually because of a subsequent rest (Example 8.15). See also Beethoven, Sonata op. 57, I, m. 39.

Rahmenanschlag

Light and shade are also produced by *Rahmenanschlag* ["framing touch"][3], as for instance in the succession *f–p*, where essentially *p* represents only a shadow—as if the first tone were to stand still within *f* and finally dissolve in the shade. (See Examples 8.16 and 8.17.) See also Beethoven, Symphony no. 3, op. 55, I, m. 83ff.

$$p \ - \ cresc. \ - \ \textit{sf} > p$$

In Example 8.18, Beethoven shows the continuation of the g^2 on the downbeat of m. 9 of var. 15 by writing a *p* at the arpeggio on the third eighth. Over this *p*, the g^2 of the first beat is connected in sound to the g^2 of the fourth and fifth eighths; thus a continuing g^2 is assumed, through which the sixty-fourths figuration runs delicately. The inserted *p* as well as the sixty-fourths rule out a *crescendo* like that of m. 1 of the variation. Not until m. 10 is there a *crescendo*— which by no means contradicts the suspension $eb^2–d^2$ (which always carries with it a $>$). This pattern more or less repeats that of mm. 1–2 of the variation (Example 8.19). In mm. 9–10, however, the *crescendo* is delayed by one measure, due to the bass diminution, and along with it the *sf*, which would be unthinkable, intolerable, above the b♭ of the bass on the downbeat of m. 10.

Rahmenanschlag also serves the diminution: the *large* note is highlighted while the *small* notes remain in the shade—a manner of playing valid for all kinds of ornaments, for trills as well as for diminutions, which can be considered embellishments in the widest sense of the word. The effect must be as if the small notes did not exist at all. One example may stand for countless others—particularly in Chopin (Example 8.20). Diminutions written in large notes should be organized in the same way (Examples 8.21, 8.22, 8.23, and 8.24). A trill should initially be attacked as if no trill were to follow— fundamentally, one is merely realizing the large writing (Example 8.25).

Example 8.16 Mozart, Symphony K. 550, II, mm. 20–23. See Schenker's comment in *The Masterwork in Music*, vol. 2, p. 84: "The arpeggio is written as demisemiquaver [grace notes] [thirty-second notes; see translator's note following]. The *p* already appears on the second crotchet (i.e., the third quaver), likewise in all parts and at all analogous places! (Only with *f p* from the first to the second crotchet will the effect in the orchestra be achieved that corresponds approximately to the following pianistic effect:

where it is essential to release the pedal at the *p*; in addition, Mozart's notation preserves the generally *piano* character of the second subject.)" [Translator's note: the British terms "minim," "crotchet," "quaver," "semiquaver," "semi-demi-quaver," etc. correspond to, respectively, half note, quarter note, eighth-note, sixteenth note, etc.]

Example 8.17 Mozart, Symphony K. 551, II, mm. 23–25

Example 8.18 Beethoven, *Eroica* Variations, op. 35, Var. 15, mm. 9–10

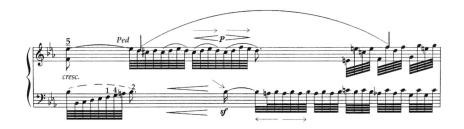

Example 8.19 Beethoven, *Eroica* Variations, op. 35, var. 15, mm. 1–2

Example 8.20 Chopin, Nocturne op. 37, no. 1, m. 19 (See Plate 3)

Example 8.21 Mozart, Symphony K. 551, II, mm. 28–29

Example 8.22 Beethoven, Sonata op. 2, no. 3, I, mm. 1–2

Example 8.23 Beethoven, Sonata op. 2, no. 3, II, m. 1

Example 8.24 Brahms, Intermezzo op. 76, no. 7, mm. 6–8

Example 8.25 Beethoven, Rondo op. 51, no. 2, m. 1

As we have seen, *Rahmenanschlag* frequently is used for repeated notes. It is a different matter when the repeated notes are to be rhetorically infused with life, as in Beethoven, Sonata op. 110, III, Recitative (see Example 5.16), or Chopin, Etude op. 25, no.1, mm. 1–2 (see Example 3.28). Here the composer points out by means of the dynamic organization that the repetitions are not to be in the shade as is the case in *Rahmenanschlag*.

Tempo and Tempo Modifications

Tempo Indication and Meter

Tempo indications as such belong to that class of performance indications from which one cannot deduce the proper way of playing. The
content itself, rather, should divulge how the required impression is to
be evoked. On the one hand, the tempo marking is the point of departure; on the other, the goal. The *allegro comodo* in the fourth movement of Brahms's Piano Quartet op. 60 in C Minor, for example: there
is no such thing as an absolute *allegro comodo*—the content of the
music alone must determine how it can serve to attain *allegro comodo*.[1]

Tempo is also related to texture: the same piece must be executed
in a different tempo depending on whether it is being played with a
heavy or less heavy sound.

One thing is essential: in a given piece, the tension must be maintained throughout. This must not result in using meter mechani-
cally to ensure the flow of the music; the means that keep the piece
in motion are of an inner nature, not of a superficially metric one.
The impulse must renew itself continually from within.

Pushing ahead—Holding back

A balanced tempo throughout a piece does not exclude freedom.
Just as in dynamics the contrast of pressure and release, light and

shade, help to unify the piece, similarly in tempo, balance is established through the contrast of pushing ahead/holding back,holding back/pushing ahead. My indications ⟶ ⟵ | ⟵ ⟶ mean: speed up—slow down | slow down—speed up. Such alternation results in the illusion of a strict tempo. The principle may be formulated as follows: what was taken away earlier must be returned later. Or in reverse: what is to be taken later must be returned in advance. This is the meaning of true *rubato*.

A particularly appropriate example of tempo modification through speeding up occurs in bars 4–6 in Beethoven's Piano Trio op. 70, no. 1, I.

If these bars were played strictly in the chosen tempo, the effect of an entirely unintended ritardando would occur. Following the fury of the staccato eighths in the preceding bars, the sparse tones would simulate a slowing down, particularly since the rests between them suggest that they should be radically separated one from another. To counter this effect it is necessary to speed up until the VI appears in m. 6; not until here is balance achieved through a corresponding holding back (notice Beethoven's explicitly added ⟩).

Or imagine a performer who played the cadence in mm. 3–4 in Example 9.1 entirely regularly, according to the beat. He would have to admit in all honesty that the effect of the cadence is weaker than if he had increased the tempo. Should he point out that the following measures require the regular tempo, one must reply that given their enhanced content, mm. 5–6 are convincing in the normal tempo without hurrying. In the two preceding measures, however, the quarter notes, given their lack of rhythmic variation, would appear rather empty and therefore weak. Thus we conclude that the desired effect requires hurrying—a requirement that notation is unable to indicate.

It follows that there are particular circumstances in composition that oblige the performer to make tempo modifications. This is to avoid a totally different effect from that intended by him and by the composer on the listener, who at all times is the object and measure of the effect. It is precisely such dissembling that can fulfill the intended effect.

Repeated notes demand hurrying on to the next downbeat (Example 9.2). Speeding up of repeated notes leads to a "root syllable," as it were:

Example 9.1 Chopin, Polonaise op. 26, no. 1, mm. 3–6

Example 9.2 Beethoven, Symphony no. 5, op. 67, I, mm. 1–2 (see Plate 3)

Chopin, Etude op. 25, no. 1, mm. 1–2

The same is true for a repeated rhythmic pattern as in the following:

Chopin, Polonaise op. 40, no. 1, m. 32

Mozart, Sonata K. 331, I, mm. 3–4

Neighboring notes, chromatics, diminutions of the lowest order want expressive treatment; without pushing ahead—holding back, this would be impossible. In Example 9.3, speeding up in the left hand at the beginning secures the passing tone for the listener as well as for the performer, who now can execute the embellishment freely. Both together result in the illusion of freely flowing rhythm, an impression brought about by the forward motion of the left hand.

The requirement that a composition's form not be exposed too nakedly frequently demands considerably quicker playing where the seam occurs (Example 9.4).

Example 9.3 Handel Suite no. 2 in F Major, I, m. 1

Example 9.4 Haydn, Sonata Hob. XVI:35, II, mm. 8–9

Example 9.5 Johann Strauss, Blue Danube Waltz, op. 314, mm. 1–2

Example 9.6 Beethoven, Sonata op. 57, II, m. 41ff. and m. 49ff.

Example 9.7 Beethoven, String Quartet op. 59, no. 2, I, mm. 39–40

Played in this way, the separate sections are pulled together, whereas without such a tempo deviation they would fall apart needlessly, compromising the texture of the form.

Even the dance-waltz traditionally demands freedom of rhythm: by holding back (Example 9.5).

It would, however, be wrong to emphasize figures of no individual significance (mere figurations or filling) by slowing down as, for instance, in Example 9.6.

However, a certain lingering is to be recommended on a trill: precisely that which the trill wants to express forces one to give that expression sufficient space. Thus the trill—like *sf, fp,* accents on weak beats (see preceding discussion), arpeggios, suspensions, etc.—belongs to those subtle means music uses to break the rigidity of motion and rhythm. Therefore even without a prescribed *ritenuto* enough time should be taken to execute the trill comfortably (Example 9.7). The retarding effect of suspension and arpeggio is based on their very nature: the suspension delays the harmony; the arpeggio, the essential melody note.

Indications such as *pesante* (heavy) and *sostenuto* (held) refer to the overall character of a formal section but do not mean a slowing down of the tempo. Thus the general direction "Pesante" in Example 9.8 a–e refers to the expression of:

$c\flat^1$ in the third quarter of m. 1;

$e\flat^1$ in the fourth quarter of m. 3;

$g\flat^1$ in the fourth quarter of m. 4;

$f\flat^1$ in the first quarter of m. 7;

$d\flat^1$ in the first quarter of m. 8.

The marking "Sostenuto" in Example 9.9 refers to f^2 in m. 1; $a\flat$–$b\flat$–$a\flat$ in m. 2; $g\flat^2$ in m. 3; $e\flat^2$ in m. 9; f^2 in m. 10; et cetera.

Frequently it is advisable to emphasize the return to the tempo after holding back by bringing the relevant beat even earlier than would be permissible in strict time (Example 9.10).

Newly Appearing Note Values

Each new rate of motion, sixteenths after eighths, thirty-seconds after sixteenths, et cetera—and vice versa—must be introduced as clearly as possible. For this purpose it is necessary to play the very

Example 9.8 Chopin, Prelude op. 28, no. 14, mm. 1, 3, 4, 7, 8

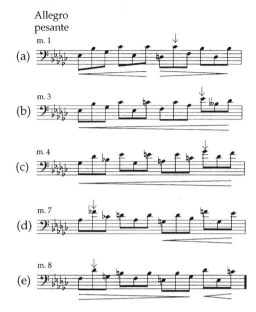

Example 9.9 Chopin, Prelude op. 28, no. 15, mm. 1–3 and 9–10

Example 9.10 Beethoven, Sonata op. 101, I, mm. 16–17

first notes of the new rhythmic pattern a little slower than the absolute strictness of the metronome would demand. The reason for this rule, which has no exception, derives from the effect on the listener: if the tempo were maintained with metronomic precision, without considering the listener, the newly introduced motion would prevent his immediate understanding precisely because of the regularity of tempo. It is thus the listener who requires a comfortable moment's lingering in order to comprehend the change of rhythm. If this is not provided for him by the performer, his ear cannot simply adjust; he gets the impression that the performer is rushing.[2] It follows that a performance in the strictest tempo does not seem thus to the listener; for psychological reasons, that which actually was metronomically perfect sounds hasty to him.

Even in midst the turmoil of the greatest passion one must not be carried away to rush or gloss over the beginning of a new rate of motion. Once the motion has been introduced, one easily can give it free rein, but always relative to the appropriate required expression (Examples 9.11, 9.12, and 9.13).

Alla breve

Alla breve ¢ refers to meter, but not, as is generally believed, to tempo. As used in earlier music, it serves to present the content in larger note values than would otherwise have been possible. Two— if not four—measures equal one, had that one been written in smaller note values (Example 9.14). One should be particularly warned against taking too fast a tempo when ¢ is combined with *Presto*. It is precisely the use of larger note values that causes the composer to write *Presto* as a precaution, since *Allegro* might be taken too slowly. It does not follow from this that *Presto* in itself implies a fast motion; it rather can be understood in connection with the mode of notation and the reasons for it as shown previously. Thus a tempo just a little faster than a simple *Allegro* would be entirely appropriate. See also Example 9.15.

Example 9.11 Beethoven, Sonata op. 2, no. 1, I, mm. 18–21

Example 9.12 Beethoven, Sonata for Piano and Violin op. 96, I, mm. 32–34

Example 9.13 Beethoven, Sonata op. 10, no. 3, III, mm. 67–68

Example 9.14 Mozart, Sonata K. 310, III, mm. 1–4

Example 9.15 J. S. Bach, *The Art of Fugue* (a) original (b) printed version

Contrapunctus: (a) (b)

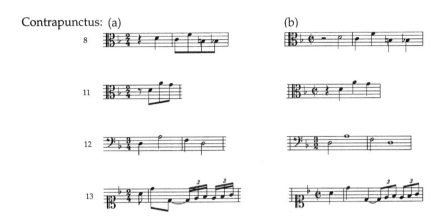

sf(p) on the Weak Beat

When an *sf(p)* occurs on a weak beat it is usually advisable to take that weak beat earlier than would be demanded in strict time; one should, as it were, fall onto the tone and balance the timing on the far side of the *sf*. The reason for this: ordinarily the bar organization gives the player no opportunity to shape the flow of time in an unusual way; an *sf* on a weak beat, however, gives the impression that the composer felt compelled to destroy the norm during a particular moment of intense emotion. It is this intense emotion that demands its equivalent on the part of the player. How could it be expressed other than by hurrying, by rushing to the weak beat?!

After the weak beat—in moving to the next strong one—one must hesitate. This slowing down serves not only to restore the regular pace but also, far more, as a contrast to the preceding rushing (Example 9.16).

Example 9.17 is an intensification of expression, versus the version without *sfp* as in m. 1.[3] In relation to this consider Example 9.18.

Example 9.16 Mozart, Sonata K. 332, I, mm. 94–100

Example 9.17 Beethoven, String Quartet op. 59, no. 1, I, m. 38

Example 9.18 Mozart, String Quartet K. 421, I, m. 34

Compare also Beethoven, Sonata op. 57, I, m. 42; or III, mm. 98, 102:

Especially noteworthy are cases in which two or more *sfs* immediately follow one another: Beethoven, Symphony no. 9, op. 125, I, mm. 31–34:

$$f \quad sf \quad sf \quad sf \quad sf$$

IV, mm. 598–600 (i.e., mm 4–6 of the Andante maestoso):

$$sf \quad sf$$

Compare also Variations op. 34, var. 1, mm. 10–11: it is as if each *sforzando* prepared the following one psychologically, as it were. To attain the desired expression in this case, it is necessary to hurry to the second *sf* [4] (Example 9.19).

Emphasis on weak beats must not by any means be avoided, whether the composer explicitly demands this or not. There are an infinite number of gradations of such emphases, up to the limits of a prescribed

$$sf, \quad fp, \quad >, \quad <>$$

and similar symbols. Least of all may they be omitted when a new motive begins on the weak beat (Examples 9.20 and 9.21). Similarly, consider Example 9.22; see also Example 3.14a.

Example 9.19 Beethoven, Variations op. 34, var. 1, mm. 10–11

Example 9.20 Mozart, String Quartet K. 387, I, m. 21. The indication *sf* was added by Schenker as elucidation! The Einstein-Novello edition has a *p*, taken from the manuscript. The facsimile of the manuscript shows a crossed-out *for* or *fp* and, as final indication, clearly *pia*. The New Mozart Edition decided on *fp*.

Example 9.21 Beethoven, Sonata for Piano and Violin op. 24, IV, mm. 1–2

Allegro ma non troppo

Example 9.22 Beethoven, Sonata op. 22, IV, mm. 1–2

Example 9.23 Beethoven, String Quartet op. 18, no. 1, II, mm. 9–11

Each such stress, whether within *piano* or *forte*, needs to be anticipated; thus the performer must be prepared to anticipate the main accent with ⟩ shadows. This gives an impetus that aids both content and form: vivid means such as this seem to set even the tiniest part of the whole into intense vibration; the content, which otherwise would simply be annihilated by the metrical pattern, lives and breathes.

In Example 9.23, the entrance in m. 2, which comes "too early," then stops, is actually written in this way by Beethoven. (In the first version of the String Quartet, both measures are the same, i.e., like the first!) Also listen to what Schindler says about Beethoven's playing of his Sonata op. 14. no. 1, I, mm. 12–13:

> With the entrance of the second theme the dialogue became sentimental and the tempo an *Andante*, but very fluctuating, as each voice received a momentary hold, approximately thus:

Example 9.24 Beethoven, Sonata op. 14, no. 1, I, mm. 22–23

Rests

A PHRASE SUCH AS Example 10.1 gives the pianist an opportunity to use a technique learned by violinists. A violinist will continue the motion of the bow through the eighth rest to the d^2 that follows after he releases the string. The pianist can produce a similar effect by using the hand's impulse after being hurled from the $f\sharp^2$ to reach the d^2. Lowering the hand because of the rest would be counterproductive and give an entirely different effect.

The opposite of this technique is the imitation of the abrupt stopping of the bow. The violinist has to use utmost precision at this instant or the sound will continue. The same is required on the piano, the thrusting-away motion being absorbed by the lower arm.

At times dissembling means must be used in the execution of rests. If, for instance, in Example 10.2 the composer writes (b) instead of (a), the player should hasten to the second half of the second beat, holding back immediately afterward. This corresponds to the compositional origin of the rest. Without hurrying and then holding back (see p. 53 ff), considering the intended expression, the effect of an unintentional *ritenuto* results. It follows that a rest is often more than it seems: it has thematic significance and is a motive in itself, which is how it must be played.[1] (See Examples 10.3 and 10.4.)

See also Beethoven, Sonata op.81a, I, mm.15–16 (end of the Introduction):

Example 10.1 Mozart, Piano Trio, K. 564, III, mm. 1–4

Allegretto

Example 10.2 C. P. E. Bach, *Sonata for Connoisseurs and Amateurs, Third Collection*, no. 2, I, mm. 13–15

Instead of:

(a)

Bach writes:

(b)

Example 10.3 Beethoven, Sonata op. 79, II, mm. 32–34

Example 10.4 Beethoven, *Coriolanus* Overture, op. 62, mm. 286–89 and 270–71

m. 286- 289   m. 270- 271

from:

Example 10.5 Beethoven, Sonata op. 81a, III, mm. 176–77

Poco andante

Example 10.6 Haydn, Sonata Hob. XVI:49, I, mm. 200–202

Frequently an increase in tempo serves to keep the tension through the rest (Examples 10.5, 10.6).

In the same sonata see II, mm. 15–17:

From an abundance of examples these may be cited:

Haydn, Symphony Hob. I: 101, II, mm. 96–98:

Schubert, Symphony No. 8, D. 759, I, mm. 61–63:

Schubert, Sonata D. 960, IV, mm. 10–11:

mm. 153–56:

Example 10.7 Beethoven, Sonata op. 27, no. 1, III, mm. 25–31

Example 10.8 Beethoven, Sonata op. 31, no. 3, II, mm. 8–9 and 35

Example 10.9 Beethoven, Sonata op. 31, no. 2, I, m. 121

A so-called *Atempause* (breathing space) generally occurs to clarify mental organization; it is a device of the synthesis. An entirely different type of rest is that which is due to limitations of the instrument, be it the piano or the orchestra, for example in large leaps, strong dynamic swells, or sudden occurrences that cannot be accomplished with mathematical precision without giving the impression of haste. Better, then to use a *Notpause* ["rest of necessity"]! Examples 10.7, 10.8, and 10.9 demonstrate such cases.

ELEVEN

The Performance of Older Music

Expression and Freedom in Older Works

The view is widespread that the richer the instrumentation, the thicker and more orchestral the piano writing, the more difficult the music will be to perform. There is, however, more and more awareness that a composition by Wagner or Richard Strauss actually is incomparably easier to perform than the earlier classics. But not too much should be read into this insight: even those who voice it for the most part are unable to give the real reason for the fact.

Frequently when a symphony by Tchaikovsky or a work of Richard Strauss—in short, a piece reverberating with brass instruments —is performed, we hear the phrase "the orchestra once again outdid itself" in conversations and reviews. But it must be said that just that sort of noise performs itself, so to speak, and that the composition in general does not even give the orchestra a chance to show if it truly can outdo itself. For pieces such as these do not confront the performer with difficulties. The masterworks, however, composed in a profound manner by our Classical composers, present problems from note to note solved by few performers. To outdo oneself here indeed would be a task worth dedicating oneself to, and with utmost passion!

In older forms—the suites of J. S. Bach, for instance—understanding the diminutions presents great problems, greater, thanks to their restless polyphony, than those in, say, a sonata movement in

Beethoven. The laws of the linear progressions are identical in both, certainly, but the diminution figurations, moving all but ceaselessly in regular note values, prevent insight, allow the mind no rest, while in a Beethoven movement already the rhetorical rests offer the performer the relief of breathing. Now even if the player can follow the meaning neither there nor here, he nonetheless moves more comfortably in the even externally more "speaking" manner of Beethoven than in the "connected" world of Bach. That is why it is harder to come to terms with Bach, to make his meaning "speak."

Expressive, rhetorical performance, however, is demanded again and again and was practiced in their own playing by J. S. Bach, C. P. E. Bach, Mozart. How curious that a nonrhetorical performance, which thus is no performance at all, can earn as much or more applause! Furthermore, a calamitous belief in progress led in music to the erroneous conclusion that expressive playing and freedom in execution can only be found in a later epoch (preferably dated from Berlioz, peaking in Liszt and Wagner), certainly post-Classical. The truth is that the very nature of the content of the works of our Classical masters, thanks to their inimitably free-flowing synthesis, lends itself to greater freedom of expression. Nothing is as wrong as today's performers—who, claiming that recent works are more intensely expressive—regard older works as being less expressive, and perform them with less freedom accordingly.[1]

Specifically the performance of Classical works must be shaped freely and expressively. All that contemporaries have reported enthusiastically about the infinitely free and colorful performances of J. S. Bach, C. P. E. Bach, Mozart and Beethoven, Mendelssohn and Brahms, all that should be taken as evidence for this fact. If one adds what can be found in essays and letters by these masters, then one cannot but become convinced that their music is performed correctly only if it is played with utmost freedom.

Improvisation: Fermatas and Cadenzas

Frequently older masterworks require the elaboration of fermatas and cadenzas. I need not point out the sad state of this ability today. Its dying out is the natural consequence of composers accustoming themselves to writing down in the most precise manner every detail that conceivably might be considered part of the composition. This custom developed out of the growing spread of dilettantism in music, which again in equal measure caused the diminishing and eventual disappearance of expertise among performers. Precisely for this reason the masters must have felt well-grounded skepticism toward the performer. And so the bitter prophecies of a C. P. E. Bach, a J. J. Quantz, have been fulfilled; the ability to improvise, to execute fermatas and cadenzas, has been lost for all time. Lost also is the skill of working out a continuo bass—something predicted no less definitely by C. P. E. Bach.

Passagework and Scales

Passages and scales, as we encounter them in older works, are, unfortunately, frequently misunderstood: as a result of the piano methods of post-Classical times, that which we call a passage was robbed of any artistic value. Thought up by their authors purely as finger exercises, these passages are devoid of any origin in the spirit. The student, no matter where he encounters them outside piano methods or etudes, involuntarily associates such passages with mere finger exercises. An example from C. P. E. Bach may elucidate this point (Example 11.1). This idea represents an entity wherein the II step is expressed in the form of a scalelike passage. Superficial players tend to forget that amid the rhetorical tonal language of the preceding and following bars, an empty fast-finger demonstration, bare of any expression, is pointless. But precisely the context of the passage should demonstrate to us that it serves as a means of expression as well.

Hereby I touch on a point of decisive significance for the character and evaluation of the excellence of our masterworks: passages and *fiorituras* are an integral part of older works and themselves share in the overall expressiveness. The great masters were great in-

Example 11. 1 C. P. E. Bach, *Sonata for Connoisseurs and Amateurs, Third Collection*, no. 2, I, mm. 19–22

strumentalists who could indulge their delight in playing all the more easily by having the ability to bring together a wealth of figurations through synthesis. Mozart was a consummate pianist and an excellent violinist; Haydn, too, was a violinist of stature; Bach was a master of the organ, the harpsichord, et cetera. Figurations literally sprang out of their imagination the more they were aware of the background, that is, of diminution. This explains the fact that frequently, the most exalted language notwithstanding—in the Adagios, for instance—our masters do not dispense with passages and ornaments. Even in his last works, Beethoven draws on a variety of figurations to serve as a means of ardent expression.

It is noticeable that even in the works of Schubert, Schumann, and Mendelssohn the delight in similar figurations and passages diminishes sadly. I say sadly since particularly the late works of Beethoven, his Piano Sonatas, his Sonatas for Piano and Violin, his Piano Trios, yes, even the Ninth Symphony and the Missa Solemnis, prove that the deepest expressiveness need not preclude instrumental effects. In this sense, the last piano sonatas of Beethoven represent the highest and noblest type of pure piano music. As mentioned earlier, Schumann could no more than Schubert or Mendelssohn find the way back to that ideal of piano art; lacking genuinely pianistic figurations, he compensated, as it were, incorporating orchestral effects into his works.

One step further was taken by Brahms, who introduced the most extensive octave playing to the piano. To be sure, this master reconquered, regarding synthesis, that high level of composition on which stood Bach, Haydn, Mozart, and Beethoven. Thus he succeeded in creating his own individual piano style in which orchestral and pianistic-polyphonic playing, with intensified expressiveness, were combined in such a way that he could dispense with the figurations and passages of Beethoven.

It was through Wagner—with his diminishing awareness of synthesis—that the foreground became encumbered by segments and components of motives too ponderous to have wings, as it were. A certain weight pressed down the motive or its parts—this was Wagner's clear intention—but the propulsion of diminution was gone. The *crescendi* in flight, the extended tones aiming at individual notes—these do not occur in Wagner's works.

Now the error was made of imposing the rendition of this weighed-down diminution on older works. They were infused with pathos—a quality incompatible with the flexibility and transparency of their diminutions. But such pathos is not appropriate to the motives and motive fragments in the works of Bach, Haydn, Mozart, et cetera; equally inappropriate is weighing down moving eighths and sixteenths, congealing in a *crescendo* from one tone to another.

Light and spirited renditions are made possible only by an overall view, by thinking ahead, thereby giving wings to the hand. The ear, too, like the eye, must offer us perspective. This ability comes from understanding the background. (No playing the way a pedestrian might walk who gropes his way from paving stone to paving stone!)

It becomes evident from all this that figurations and passages in the works of older masters should be given the dignity of the most genuine and beautiful expression—if, that is, one does not intend to credit a present-day Czerny with them!

TWELVE

On Practicing

ASSUMING KNOWLEDGE AND MASTERY of the instrument, the study of significant, good compositions must begin immediately with their expressive performance. A musical person, having reached a certain level, does not need to practice in the sense of finger exercises and etudes; such practicing only leads back to these very exercises, to these very etudes—a world not worth reaching. In a world worthy of the effort, such studies do not guarantee security.

By no means can everything be practiced! Certain difficulties, experienced by the composer himself, can only be borne and overcome through the *spirit* of the performer, not by practicing. A distant world from that of practicing! Virtuosos are defeated by such passages, and finger exercises are of no avail. Only the spirit can find the way: it knows how to reduce the problem to a simple formula, thereby eliminating it. Examples occur in Beethoven's Piano Trio op. 97, in the octave leaps, m. 104ff., at the beginning of the development of the first movement (Example 12.1a), in the fourth-movement octave arpeggios, mm. 36, 38, 40ff., which are embellished with slurs (Example 12.1b), as well as in the final bars; in Sonata op. 109, III, var. 6, m. 25ff. in the thirty-seconds of the left hand (Example 12.2), and in Sonata op. 27, no. 1, II, m. 89ff.:

as well as in III (the Allegro vivace), m. 58ff.

instead of the reverse

.

Example 12. 1 Beethoven, Piano Trio op. 97 (a) I, m. 104ff.; (b) IV, mm. 40–43

Example 12. 2 Beethoven, Sonata op. 109, III, var. 6, mm. 25–26

Example 12. 3 Beethoven, Sonata op. 90, I, m. 55ff.

 etc.

Technical difficulties in a work of art can be equated with the difficulties fate brings in life—but they must be generated by the synthesis. That is: the composer may not throw in a technical problem merely to show himself and the performer in the pose of a musician easily overcoming difficulties—such pieces are generally written by the virtuoso-composers. The difficulties must in a sense confront the composer himself, so that he is obliged to muster true spiritual and ethical strength rather than vanity to overcome them. When, for example, Beethoven in Sonata op. 90, I, second theme, m. 55ff. puts the accompaniment in tenths (Example 12.3), it is as though he himself had run across a problem that he now has to overcome with utmost fervor. Editors who suggest a simplification in such a spot thereby deprive it of its real meaning. Simplifications such as dividing figurations between the two hands fall into the same category.[1]

———

Each work of art has only *one* true rendition—its own, particular one —etudes are of no help whatsoever here. This is true even of fingering: it is unseemly to use ingenious fingerings in pieces and places that do not call for such ingenuity. Every piece has its own special fingering, its own special dynamics. All practicing of studies misses the point, as fingering, dynamics, and position of hand and fingers in any particular piece are not applicable to any other. That is why the art of performance is unattainable for the many who, from incompetence, attempt to get by with an absolute model for fingering, dynamics, and hand position.

———

With the so-called English action,[2] perfect evenness of touch has arrived. Simultaneously, music training has for decades striven for perfect evenness also of the fingers. Thus we are faced with evenness of fingers and keys. We could be pleased by this development if—what irony!—precisely the opposite were not the crux of the matter: unevenness! The fingers, by nature uneven, must play unevenly; all effort in practicing is in vain if it does not aim at unevennesses in performance.

———

The synthesis of a masterwork presents extraordinary difficulties to the performer. Its demands cannot be avoided; they even take precedence over the best finger technique, and only insight can lead the way. By no means must tempo alone be allowed to play the decisive role; it can never replace insight. Often one deludes oneself by imagining that a unified conception can be attained by fast playing; but speed only evades the issue, for by avoiding the demands of synthesis through speed, indeed, one obscures the interconnections.

The purpose of all practicing must therefore be to practice the conceptual demands until the desired tempo has been reached. Up to then, the mechanics of playing must be subordinated and the tempo held back accordingly in order to avoid the hand's automatic carrying out of an unintentional effect. Once the conceptual requirements have been truly assimilated, then and only then can one entrust one's technical equipment to them. At that point, even the quickest tempo will be within easy reach.

———

Lazy players play fast—this is no paradox! They are too lazy to go through the many motions necessary for playing expressively. Such players "are played," as it were, by the tones.

———

In the end, what matters is the ability to hear and evaluate all the effects of one's own playing; this is surely the most difficult task of all! If one is still struggling with finger control and uses up all nervous energy in achieving the correct finger motion, then nothing is left to control that which the fingers produce. Only one who speedily produces into the fingers, so to speak, gains sufficient time and energy to judge the effect as well.

Only if the performer is fully aware of the desired effect will he be able to convey it. This effect then serves to justify any means he might use to produce it. The psychology of this fact is so compelling that even mistakenly desired effects become tolerable when the performer conveys them with awareness and conviction. Only that result which the player produces involuntarily, with no notion of why and wherefore, is rejected.

Physical gestures as a means of expression belong here as well— similar to the arm movements of a string player or the breathing technique of a wind player. A performer cannot possibly produce the composer's intended result if he ignores these gestures. Even unseen by the listener, the player's gesture will convey its effect if only he uses it.

———

If the performance is to express the content in its entirety, then utmost daring and total mastery of the technical and spiritual means are essential. Of what does this mastery consist? Of nothing else but the elimination of any anxiety. Gradually the performer must come to realize that anxiety is entirely unjustified. If he recalls from his earliest piano lessons that the left hand did not want to move separately from the right and nonetheless was trained to independence, if he further remembers the greater difficulties encountered in the independent motions of several elements that he mastered nevertheless, thus may he draw the reassuring conclusion that musical energy is ever ready to expand. Eventually it learns to make each instant precious and meaningful. May the pianist therefore not lose heart but have faith in his own ability, by means of the greatest variety of hand and arm motions, by the most manifold gradations, to infuse the tones with genuine life.

Appendix A

On the Technique of the Piano in Particular

[In A, chapter 3 is followed by one titled "On the Technique of the Piano in Particular." Its publication in full is planned in a different context. Here follows a summary of its content.]

The arm must be used as a tool in its entire length in such a way that it passes the instructions of the nerves on to the fingers without interference—in a channel, as it were. Thus any position of hand and arm is to be avoided that contradicts the law of gravity. Any other position that requires a special effort would tire the hand and arm. The shoulder, elbow, and wrist function as nodal points, which secure the steady state of rest of the arm; this means that the arm can be brought into such a relaxed state that all three nodal points remain in their natural position according to gravity. The keyboard, conversely, is the point of support without which the arm would drop down.

The vertical motion of the arm is countered by the horizontal one of the hand, which moves from right to left. But this horizontal direction also requires an effort that would tire the arm were the player not to find relaxing moments. These consist of the release of the natural weight of the hand in pressure on the keys. The composition must be the decisive factor in finding which places are appropriate for the release of pressure. The freed hand is then enabled to move from one point of pressure to the next in a flying motion; to and from this point the lightest mobility prevails.

An analogy to the human respiratory organs lies at hand: just as the tension of inhaling is balanced by the relaxation of exhaling, similarly every tension of hand and arm position must be followed by relaxation. Thus the elbow in a certain sense is the mouth of the arm. When the elbow has been brought to rest, the arm has by analogy exhaled. The equivalent of the singer's taking a breath is the pianist's attacking the key from a certain height above it. He must take sufficient time for the necessary preparatory hand motion. Inasmuch as the mode of notation knows nothing of this we have the situation described in chapter 2, where there appears to be a contradiction between mode of notation and execution that is only resolved in the effect. (The absence of such preparatory rests differentiates organ technique from piano technique in a very characteristic manner.)

Appendix B

On the Degeneracy of the Virtuoso

[The manuscript of A closes with a chapter "On the Degeneracy of the Virtuoso." It takes up the idea developed in chapter 2 on the union of creation and re-creation. Here follows a summary of its content.]

In an earlier epoch, only that performer who performed his own compositions stepped before the public. The development of music depended on this identity. Handel, J. S. Bach, C. P. E. Bach, Mozart, Beethoven, Mendelssohn, and Brahms were also the foremost virtuosos of their time. If, however, Haydn, Schubert, or Schumann did not appear before the public to the same extent, their occasional performances proved sufficiently that they, too, would have been at the pinnacle of reproducing musicians had they not been prevented from demonstrating this ability more frequently by circumstances.

The identity of production and reproduction was lost over the course of time. More and more, people came to consider a purely reproductive ability as equal to productive ability. This state of affairs, caused by lack of talent, led to the attempt by thousands—be it from vanity, be it from financial greed—to appear before the public. Since they lacked true ability in the earlier sense, they made a virtue of their defect and declared the profession of virtuoso as organically necessary as that of composer. The profession of virtuoso, based on a lie, prevailed and attained the recognition of artistic justification.

Still at the close of the eighteenth and at the beginning of the nineteenth century there were virtuosos with sufficient ability to compose and improvise so that one could speak of an integrated whole, if to a lesser extent. Muzio Clementi may be named as an example; with his "Gradus ad Parnassum" a rank of composer was assured him such as can hardly be granted later, be it to Thalberg, Tausig, or Bülow. In the world of etudes, Clementi is only surpassed by Chopin. Liszt, in his etudes, however, added elements to the music that, beside much that is excellent and original, tended to destroy rather than develop it. Still in recent times [written 1911] Anton Rubinstein, d'Albert, Busoni, and Paderewski to a certain degree have achieved a unified whole. All the sadder for the thousands who are brought to the stages of all the world. The economics of the concert agencies, once in motion, demand more artistic sacrifices daily. Most virtuosos who go onstage prove themselves artistically not up to the works they are performing; they speak the tonal language like a badly learned foreign tongue. In order to survive in the battle at competition, they grasp for unallowed means of false effect that they want to pass off as marks of their own individuality. In truth, they are incapable of offering the spiritual equivalent of the composer's written-down note symbols. They are outside the sphere of the composer's living vision; they are merely slaves of engraver and hand position.

The more irresponsibly the virtuosos treat their profession, the easier it is to enter it. In the fight for survival, the many, too many, must attempt to outdo one another by dishonest means: they must learn the longest programs; they attempt to play ever louder, ever faster. Banished from a paradise of union of production and reproduction, a lie avenges itself on them.

Notes

Chapter 1

1. Mozart to his father from Mannheim, January 17th, 1778: "And wherein consists the art of playing prima vista? In this: in playing the piece in the time in which it ought to be played, and in playing all the notes, appoggiaturas and so forth, exactly as they are written and with the appropriate expression and taste, so that you might think the performer had composed it himself." *The Letters of Mozart and His Family.* Translated and edited by Emily Anderson (London: Macmillan Press, 1966). First American revised edition New York: W. W. Norton, 1985, p. 449.

Beethoven to Tomaschek, 1814: "It has always been acknowledged that the greatest pianists were also the greatest composers, but how did they play? Not like the pianists of today, who only run up and down the keyboard with passages they have learned by heart—putch, putch, putch! What does that mean? Nothing! The real piano virtuosos, when they played, gave us something interconnected, a whole. When it was written down it could be accepted as a well-composed work. That was piano playing, the rest is nothing!" *Beethoven: The Man and the Artist As Revealed in His Own Words.* Translated and edited by Henry Edward Krehbiel (New York: Dover, 1964), p. 37.

C. P. E. Bach, *Essay on the True Art of Playing Keyboard Instruments,* chap. 3, § 2: "But wherein does good performance consist? In nothing other than the ability to make musical ideas perceptible to the ear according to their true content and emotion through playing or singing. By variety herein, one and the same idea can appear so changed that one can barely sense that the two are identical." (Translated by I.S.)

Chapter 2

1. Compare Schenker in *Beethoven's Ninth Symphony*, pp. 8–10: "In appearance, my performance instructions stand in contradiction to Beethoven's own orthography—that is, to the way he has written down the content. But this apparent contradiction resolves itself as soon as I explain the nature of the orthography. Specifically, it is not the task of the orthography, as is generally believed and taught, to provide the player with perfectly definite means for achieving effects allegedly specified and attainable only through precisely these means, but rather to arouse in his mind, in an *a priori* manner, specific effects, leaving it up to him to choose freely the appropriate means for their attainment. It is therefore incorrect to see in the orthography nothing more than the definite specifications of equally definite means, and to take it literally in this sense. What is correct, rather, is that the orthography on the contrary allows the player free rein concerning the means to be employed, just so long as they actually do attain that definite effect which alone was meant to be expressed by the orthography. In short: orthography announces and seeks effects, but says nothing at all about the means of producing them!

"From this standpoint, therefore, a legato slur, for example, expresses first and foremost merely the desire for the effect of a legato, without indicating in what way it is supposed to be achieved; and it is accordingly wrong to associate—invoking the orthography as the allegedly authentic wish of the composer—with a legato slur the conception of only one, completely definite, manner of execution from the outset.

"Or—to speak of dynamic markings as well—if the composer writes a *p*, for example, he wants it to express only the desire for the effect of a *p*: far from specifying any absolute quantity, however, he leaves it to the player to seek and express this effect by taking into account various circumstances, such as the instrument, the register of the melodic content (high or low), and so forth. Under certain circumstances, therefore, the effect of a *p* will be produced in, for example, a higher register by a dynamic quantity which, if measured by an absolute standard, would have to count as *mf* or indeed even as *f.*

"A second example: an *sf* notated by the composer signifies, again, the desire only for the effect of an *sf*, but leaves to the discretion of the player himself to choose from among the numerous means of production the one which, in the given situation, is the most desirable with respect to effect."

Chapter 3

1. J. Fr. Reichardt on C. P. E. Bach's keyboard playing:"Herr Bach plays a rather slow, singing Adagio not only with the most touching expression, putting to shame many instrumentalists who could approximate a singing voice with much less effort . . ." J. Fr. Reichardt, *Briefe eines aufmerksamen Reisenden, die Musik betreffend,* vol. 2 (Frankfurt and Breslau:1776), p. 16. (Translated by H.E.)

.

M. Claudius to H. W. von Gerstenberg: "His [C. P. E. Bach's] playing of an Adagio cannot be better described than, if I may humbly ask you to imagine, an orator who has not memorized his speech but rather is filled by its content, does not rush to utter something but rather calmly lets wave after wave stream out of the fullness of his soul, without any artificiality of manner." B. Engelke, "Gerstenberg und die Musik seiner Zeit." In *Zeitschrift d. Ges. f. Schleswig-Holsteinische Geschichte,* vol. 56. p. 432. (Kiel, 1927). (Translated by I.S.)

2. Compare Schenker's note to the Rondo of Sonata op. 53: "The intention of Beethoven's long pedals, which take no account of dissonant passing chords or mixtures, is a spiritual, almost transcendental, binding-together of larger groups, which his instrument also favored (cf. op. 31, no. 2, I, mm. 143–148 and 153–158). On modern instruments one may try to achieve this effect by half-pedaling at the passing harmonies (mm. 3, 7, 11, 15, etc.), a kind of legatissimo of the pedal, comparable to legato playing in general." Beethoven, *Complete Piano Sonatas,* vol. 2, p. 385.

3. "The term *diminution* means embellishment in a general broad sense. It has nothing to do with diminution meaning 'repetition in smaller note values'. . ." Footnote of E. Oster in Schenker, *Free Composition,* p. 93.

Chapter 5

1. The term "portamento" has come to mean many things to many people over the centuries, musicians and writers on music alike—not to mention its frequent confusion with the similar-sounding term "portato." Fortunately, we do not have to enter into a discussion of this matter, since we have Schenker's own definition, as explained in *Counterpoint,* vol. 1, pp. 90–92 and 350–52.

Schenker equates "portamento" with "port de voix," thereby indicating its origin in the human voice (and, by analogy, string instruments). It has the "function of actually filling out the large leap(s) at least in part" by sliding from one pitch to another. Although such a technique appears not to be possible on the piano, Schenker demonstrates in examples from Bach, Handel, and Brahms (similar to those shown here as Examples 5.1, 5.4, 5.6, and 5.9) that "a ligature, that is, a retention of tones . . . throws into relief the degree of tension caused by the leaps," which "has the following effect: after the completed leap, the initial tone from which the leap departs sounds together with the goal of the leap; thus the interval is much more clearly presented to the ear than if the leap were to occur 'naked' (that is, as a simple succession)."

Schenker points out that "the portamento produced on the piano in this way is nevertheless different from that executed by the singer or violinist, since they are not content merely to indicate the distance between the beginning and end of the interval, but traverse the space itself with a glissando. However, it would be incorrect to attribute the ligature, as is generally done, to the tonal poverty of the keyboard instrument and its constant need for filling-in. On the contrary, this notation must be understood as an original and autonomous poetic intention to present an interval in the form of a portamento [on the keyboard], even though only within the limits of an instrument which, indeed, does not permit a gliding-through of space of the interval, but which makes it possible to mark beginning and end in its own original way through a peculiar amalgam of juxtaposition and super-imposition (simultaneity) [of pitches]."

Schenker further notes that "ligature-tones do not constitute voices in the obbligato sense; instead of a real ligature, which conceptually would have to imply one and the same voice, only an inauthentic and apparent ligature between two different voices is notated in the above examples. It is a ligature peculiar to the piano, and this cannot be changed: an original notation that . . . strives . . . to stimulate and compel the player to achieve portamento expression." He then gives an example that according to his view "reflects exactly the principal effect of a real portamento, that is, the gliding of pitches through the space [of the leap]" (Example 5.N1). He concludes that such a "written-out legatissimo which, in this form, is endemic to the keyboard instrument alone" can appropriately be used frequently "in performing keyboard pieces in whatever epoch (including classical and post-classical works) . . . even where it is not expressly notated . . . but merely implied by the context of the passage." *Counterpoint*, vol. 1, pp. 88–91.

2. Compare Handel's Suite no. 7 in both versions (Example 5.N2). Compare also Beethoven's remark on the Cramer etudes, which he intended to publish (Example 5.N3). "The setting is in four parts throughout. The melody is in the upper voice, as can be seen from the notation (a). Even were it notated as follows,(b), the first note of each group would have to be accentuated and held. The inner voice, e^1c^2, f^1c^2, g^1c^2, etc., may not be played on the same dynamic level as the upper voice. The meter is trochaic." J. B. Cramer, *21 Etuden für Klavier*, no. 5, p. 10. Edited by H. Kann (Vienna: Universal Edition, 1974).

Example 5.N1 Handel, Suite no. 5, Air, Double IV

Example 5.N2 Handel, Suite no. 7, Second Collection, Allemande,
mm. 1–2: (a) later and final version, (b) first, earlier version

(a)

(b)

Example 5.N3 Cramer, *21 Etudes*, no. 5, m. 1

(a)   (b)

Chapter 7

1. For comments on the role of fingering as tool of interpretation and
performance see C. Schachter, Introduction to Schenker's edition of
Beethoven, *Complete Piano Sonatas*, pp. viii–ix.

2. Compare Friedrich Wieck's remark about Beethoven's playing "with
compact fingers." In "Signale," 1873, vol. 57, reprinted in F. Kerst, *Erinnerungen
an Beethoven*, vol. 2 (Stuttgart: J. Hoffmann, 1913), p. 158. Also compare the
remark of Beethoven on one of his own exercises: "keeping the hand as
closed as possible." G. Nottebohm, *Zweite Beethoveniana* (Leipzig: Rieter-
Biedermann, 1887), p. 362.

3. Particularly instructive are Chopin, Etude op. 25, no. 6, and no. 1 of
Three New Etudes; Schumann, *Concert Studies on Caprices by Paganini*, op. 10;
and Brahms, *51 Exercises*.

4. By "long" Schenker refers to those fingerings in which the passing
under of 1 or the crossing over of 3 or 4 is avoided as much as possible;
"short" fingerings are those in which the passing under or crossing over is

used more than would actually be necessary. Schenker recommends the long fingerings in Example 7.5 in order to let the hand demarcate the fifths that are realized in the run; the short fingering of Example 7.6 is appropriate to the final bravura figure; that of Example 7.7 lets the hand emphasize the circling of the neighboring notes around the main note.

Chapter 8

1. "He [Beethoven] was especially concerned about touch and its double significance: the actual, physical touch and the psychological one, to which Clementi drew attention. By the latter he meant the sound intensity sensed before the finger touches the key. Anyone unfamiliar with this phenomenon will never hear a soulful *Adagio.*" A. Schindler, *Beethoven*, part 2, 3d ed. (Münster: 1860), p. 237. (Translated by I.S.)

2. Schenker writes in his *J. S. Bach's Chromatic Fantasy and Fugue*, p. 66: "I should, indeed I must, take this opportunity to mention the following passage from a letter by Brahms (as imparted by Franz Fridberg in the *Vossische Zeitung* of April 3, 1907), discussing the opening bars of Brahms's String Quintet in G Major: "You may tell him [the cellist] he has every right to demand that, starting in the third and fourth measures, at least the two violins should merely feign their *f*! Thus they can favor him with a really nice *mf*; he can repay them later in the movement with a most beautiful *p*." Fridberg goes on to relate a conversation in which Brahms took part: "During a discussion of the various gradations of *piano* and *forte*, I heard Brahms assert that *piano* could exist even within *forte*. When someone ventured to find this contradictory, Brahms cut him off mid-word with 'nonsense,' opened a newspaper that was on the table, and took no further part in the conversation."

3. The term *Rahmenanschlag*, literally translated as "framing touch," refers to a kind of touch that brings greater emphasis to certain notes in order to distinguish these, usually the carriers of the main melodic line, from the lighter "embellishing" tones that are being framed, as it were. (See also Plate 3, showing Schenker's descriptive sketch as well as Example 8.20.)

Chapter 9

1. Brahms repeatedly changed the tempo indications in the manuscript: first he wrote "Presto," then "Tempo giusto," then "un poco presto"—and finally the printed version, "allegro comodo."

2. According to Schindler, Beethoven's execution of Sonata op. 14, no. 2, I, m.47ff. had the effect of an "Andantino, as eighth notes suddenly followed thirty-seconds and appeared slower; actually the tempo continues" (Example 9.N1). See A. Schindler, *Beethoven*, 1st ed. Münster, 1840. Not contained in later editions. Reprinted with commentary by H. Schenker in *Dreiklang*, vol. 8/9 (November 1937/February 1938), pp. 190ff.

A similar effect can be noticed in Beethoven's Sonata op. 81a, I, m. 213ff.; the close in m. 223ff., after the eighths in m. 213ff., even brings whole notes:

3. Compare also Schenker in *The Masterwork in Music*, vol. 3, p. 64, about Beethoven's Symphony no. 3, op. 55, I, m. 186ff.:

"The bass line, despite the *ff*, is conceived in terms of *espressivo* and should be played accordingly. The wind at this point pass through *staccato* crochets as if they were *piano* towards the dotted minims in bars 188–9 and 192–3, which, now played *ff*, introduce into the four-bar phrases a kind of syncopated rhythm. A sorrowful excitement is required for the bass *sf* in the following passage (bar 198 ff.); in the orchestra this can only be achieved through personal or soloistic effort." (See Example 9.N2.)

4. See C. Czerny, *Die Kunst des Vortrags* (Vienna: A. Diabelli, 1842), Chap. 2, p. 39: "In the following [Example 9.N3], the *sf* have to follow one another fast, with strength."

Example 9.N1 Beethoven, Sonata op. 14, no. 2, I, m. 47ff.

Example 9.N2 Beethoven, Symphony no. 3, op. 55, I, mm. 186 and 198

Example 9.N3 Beethoven, Sonata op. 2, no. 3, IV, mm. 119–122

Chapter 10

1. One truly magnificent example of the use of rests in serving the synthesis is the close of the Funeral March in Beethoven's Symphony no. 3, II, m. 238ff. (Example 10.N1), about which Schenker writes in *The Masterwork in Music,* vol. 3, p. 41: "The last c^1 is due on the strong beat of bar 238. Suddenly, in the midst of a profound silence, we are surprised by a *pp* stroke on the timpani; c^1 appears, but only on the weak beat. At the same time this note marks the start of the break-up of the diminution of bars 1–8. Already the first third-progression in bars 239–40 (= bars 1–2) comes to a halt, a crotchet rest separating d^1 from the final note, $e\flat^1$. The content of bars 3–4 is compressed into the weak beat of bar 240 and the strong beat of bar 241; it is as if the notes were beginning to breathe faster, notes which can no longer be sustained in the earlier, relaxed manner. The same is the case on the weak beats of bars 241 and 242, where bars 5–6 huddle together. By bar 241 there is no longer enough strength to include a d^1 at the start of the ascending arpeggiation (see the rest on the fifth semiquaver [sixteenth]), or to introduce $a\flat^1$ on the strong beat of bar 243. Thus the original relationships are distorted right up to the end. We bury the corpse of the first diminution stripped of its metrical and rhythmic soul." And further, ibid., p. 66: "The last timpani note in bar 238 prepares the c^1 of violin I, with which both the final third-progression ends and the disintegration of bars 1–8 begins. This disintegration can only be executed if violin I carries the motives across the rests, thus as it were painfully experiencing in the flesh what is signified by the falling apart of notes that originally belonged together. The quavers $e\flat^1$–c^1 in bar 240 require a $>$, as do the demisemiquavers $e\flat^1$–d^1 in bar 241, the crotchet $a\flat^1$ in bar 242 and, finally, the semiquaver figures in bars 243 and 244. Avoid, in any case, the ugly *staccato* that is everywhere to be heard; it wholly contradicts the final expiry of the idea."

Example 10.N1 Beethoven, Symphony no. 3, op. 55, II, mm. 238ff.

Chapter 11

1. In A there follows a longer digression, summarized here: The beginning of all music is chaos and disorder. Whereas in exotic nations it remained in this condition, increasing polyphony in the West necessitated bringing a solid rhythmic organization to the contrapuntally moving voices, in order to enable them—no paradox!—to move freely. In Classical music we find the happiest balance of musical content and number of voices; this allows the greatest possible freedom of performance. The following epoch brought a considerable increase in the number of voices— without a corresponding increase of content!—but just thereby diminishing the freedom of the individual voices. The many, too many, performance directives in the score, which aim at shaping the movement of voices freely, do little to help if the content is unfree and in contradiction to the too large number of voices.

Chapter 12

1. Compare Schenker's footnote to Beethoven's Sonata op. 57, I, m. 227ff., in which he points out that Beethoven specifically requests the passage to be played by one hand. The fingering in brackets—which divides the arpeggio between the hands—is only for an extreme case. Beethoven, *Complete Piano Sonatas,* vol. 2, p. 428. See also Example 7.2.

2. First introduced by the piano maker Broadwood, the "English action," through innovations in the key and hammer interaction as well as in the escapement, gave the piano a richer sound and a deeper, more reliable action. It gradually replaced the lighter "Viennese action" throughout Europe in the late nineteenth century. (I.S.)

Selected Bibliography with Annotations

Works of Heinrich Schenker

Beethovens Neunte Symphonie. Vienna: Universal Edition, 1912. (*Beethoven's Ninth Symphony.* Translated and edited by J. Rothgeb. New Haven: Yale University Press, 1992.)

Beethovens Sämtliche Klaviersonaten. Vienna: Universal Edition, 1923. Revised edition by Erwin Ratz, Vienna: Universal Edition, 1947. (Beethoven, *Complete Piano Sonatas.* Reprint of the edition from 1921–23, with an introduction by Carl Schachter. New York: Dover, 1975.)

Ein Beitrag zur Ornamentik. Vienna: Universal Edition, 1904 and 1908. (*A Contribution to the Study of Ornamentation.* Translated by H. Siegel. *Music Forum*, vol. 4, New York: Columbia University Press, 1976.)

Erläuterungsausgabe der letzten fünf Sonaten Beethovens. Vienna: Universal Edition
 op. 109, published 1913
 op. 110, published 1914
 op. 111, published 1915
 op. 101, published 1920
Revised edition by O. Jonas, Vienna: Universal Edition, 1970–71.

Der Freie Satz. Vienna: Universal Edition, 1935 Revised and edited by O. Jonas, Vienna: Universal Edition, 1956. (*Free Composition.* Translated and edited by E. Oster. New York: Longman, 1979.)

J. S. Bach, Chromatische Fantasie und Fuge. Vienna: Universal Edition, 1909. Revised edition by O. Jonas, Vienna: Universal Edition, 1969. (*J. S. Bach's Chromatic Fantasy and Fugue.* Translated and edited by H. Siegel. New York: Schirmer Books, 1984.)

"Ein Kommentar zu Schindler, Beethovens Spiel betreffend." *Dreiklang*,
    vol. 8/9, November 1937/February 1938, p. 190 ff.
Kontrapunkt, vol. 1, Stuttgart and Berlin: J. G. Cottasche Buchhandlung
    Nachfolger, 1910; vol. 2, Vienna: Universal Edition, 1922.(*Counterpoint*.
    Translated and edited by J. Rothgeb and Jurgen Thym, edited by
    J. Rothgeb. New York: Schirmer Books, 1987.)
Das Meisterwerk in der Musik. Munich: Drei Masken Verlag
        Jahrbuch I, published 1925
        Jahrbuch II, published 1926
        Jahrbuch III, published 1930
    (*The Masterwork in Music*, 3 vols., edited by W. Drabkin, Cambridge:
    Cambridge University Press
        vol. 1, published 1994
        vol. 2, published 1996
        vol. 3, published 1997)
Der Tonwille, 10 issues. Vienna: A. Gutmann Verlag, 1910–24. Reprint Hild-
    esheim: G. Olms, 1990.

Related Works

Oswald Jonas, "Die Kunst des Vortrags nach Heinrich Schenker." *Musik-
    erziehung*, vol. 15, 1962, pp. 122–129.
Oswald Jonas, "Heinrich Schenker und grosse Interpreten." *Österreichische
    Musikzeitschrift*, 19 (1964), pp. 584-89. This essay treats the critical inter-
    change between Schenker and musicians such as J. Joachim, K. Straube,
    J. Messchaert, P. Casals, and W. Furtwängler, among others.

Even more source material for Schenker's opinion of contemporary in-
terpreters is contained in the following basic work: Hellmut Federhofer,
*Heinrich Schenker. Nach Tagebüchern und Briefen in der Oswald Jonas Memorial
Collection*. Hildesheim: G. Olms, 1985.

The music reviews that Schenker published between 1891 and 1901 in
various periodicals are collected in Hellmut Federhofer, *Heinrich Schenker
als Essayist und Kritiker*, Hildesheim: G. Olms, 1990.

On the significance of fingering or interpretation, see the perceptive remarks by Carl Schachter in his introduction to the reprint of Schenker's edition of Beethoven, *Complete Piano Sonatas*.

The relationship between the "levels" of musical structure and performance is discussed by Charles Burkhart in an interesting essay, "Schenker's Theory of Levels and Musical Performance," in *Aspects of Schenkerian Theory*, edited
by David Beach, New Haven: Yale University Press, 1983, pp. 95–112.

A most valuable study, "Heinrich Schenker as an Interpreter of Beethoven's Piano Sonatas," was published by William Rothstein in *19th-Century
Music*, vol. 7, no. 1. (Summer 1984), pp. 3–28. The author quotes and comments on then-unpublished material from *Vortrag* and relates it to Schenker's
annotations in his own copy of the Beethoven sonatas.

and comments on then-unpublished material from *Vortrag* and relates it to Schenker's annotations in his own copy of the Beethoven sonatas.

Although it has no direct connection with Schenker, let me point out a particularly noteworthy book: Jean-Jacques Eigeldinger, *Chopin vu par ses élèves*, *Neuchâtel*: Editions de la Baconnière, 1970 and 1979 (*Chopin: Pianist and Teacher As Seen by His Pupils*, edited by R. Howat, Cambridge: Cambridge University Press, 1986). This book is "a sort of handbook to Chopin's teaching methods, and consequently to his aesthetic beliefs." Its agreement in nearly all points with Schenker's *The Art of Performance* is surprising—but perhaps less so if one recalls the influence Chopin's student Karol Mikuli, director of the conservatory in Lemberg (currently L'viv, Ukraine), had on the young Schenker. This book is a superb supplement and confirmation of the one before us; it is recommended highly to the reader.

Index of Musical Examples